# Adult Coloring Book
## Female Beauty

## 60 Relaxing And Stress Relieving Patterns

Coloring Books For Adults

Female Beauty Series

Volume 1

Illustrator:

Talanova Liudmila Coloring Books

# *Disclaimer*

*All rights reserved. No part of this publication or the information in it may be quoted from or reproduced in any form by means such as printing, scanning, photocopying or otherwise without prior written permission of the copyright holder.*

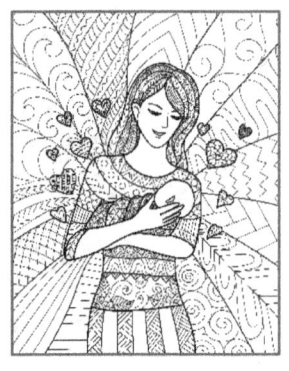 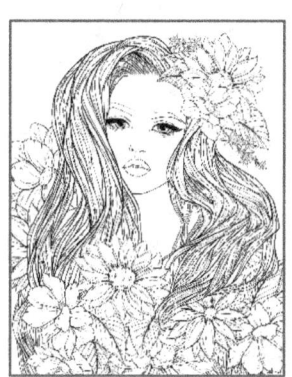 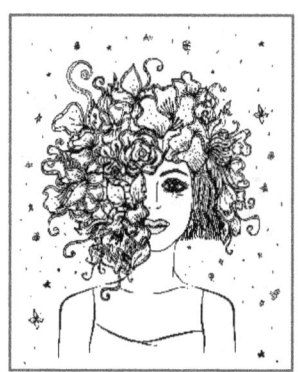

Copyright © 2019 Talanova Liudmila Coloring Books
All rights reserved.

PUBLISHED BY TALANOVA LIUDMILA COLORING BOOKS.

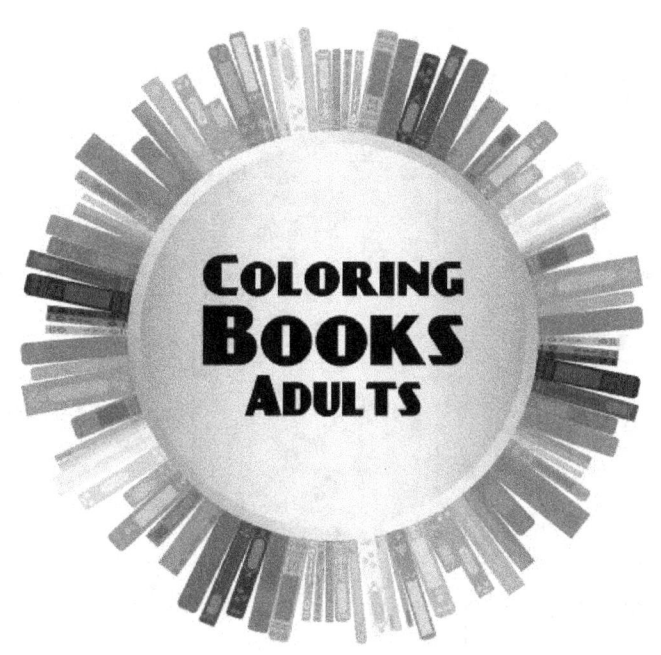

# COLORING BOOK
# BELONGS TO:

_____

_____

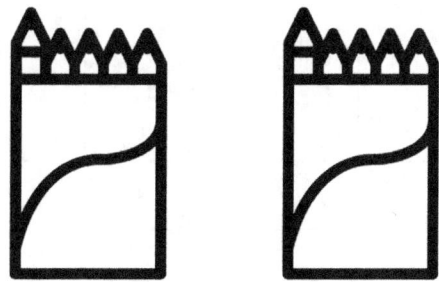

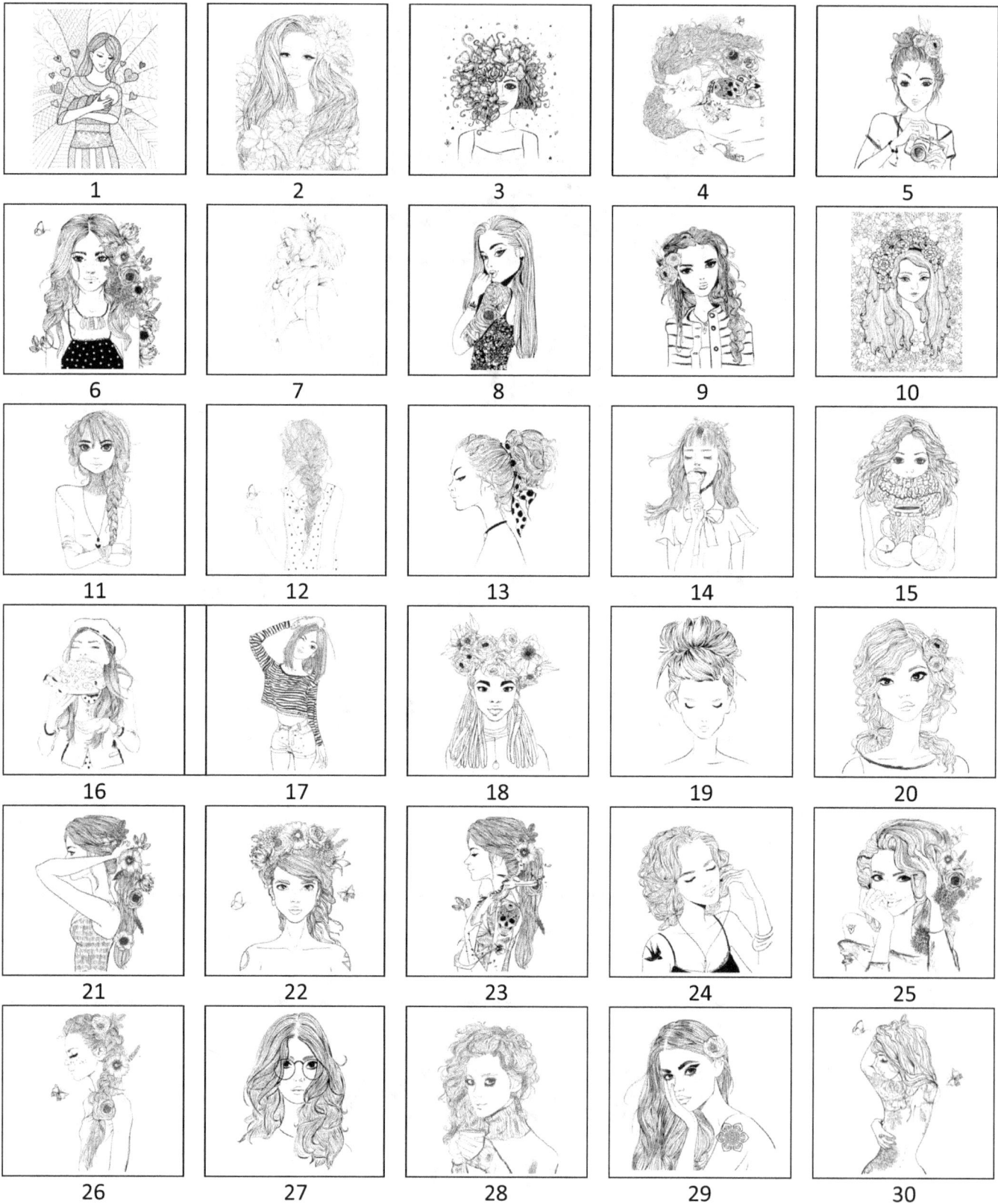

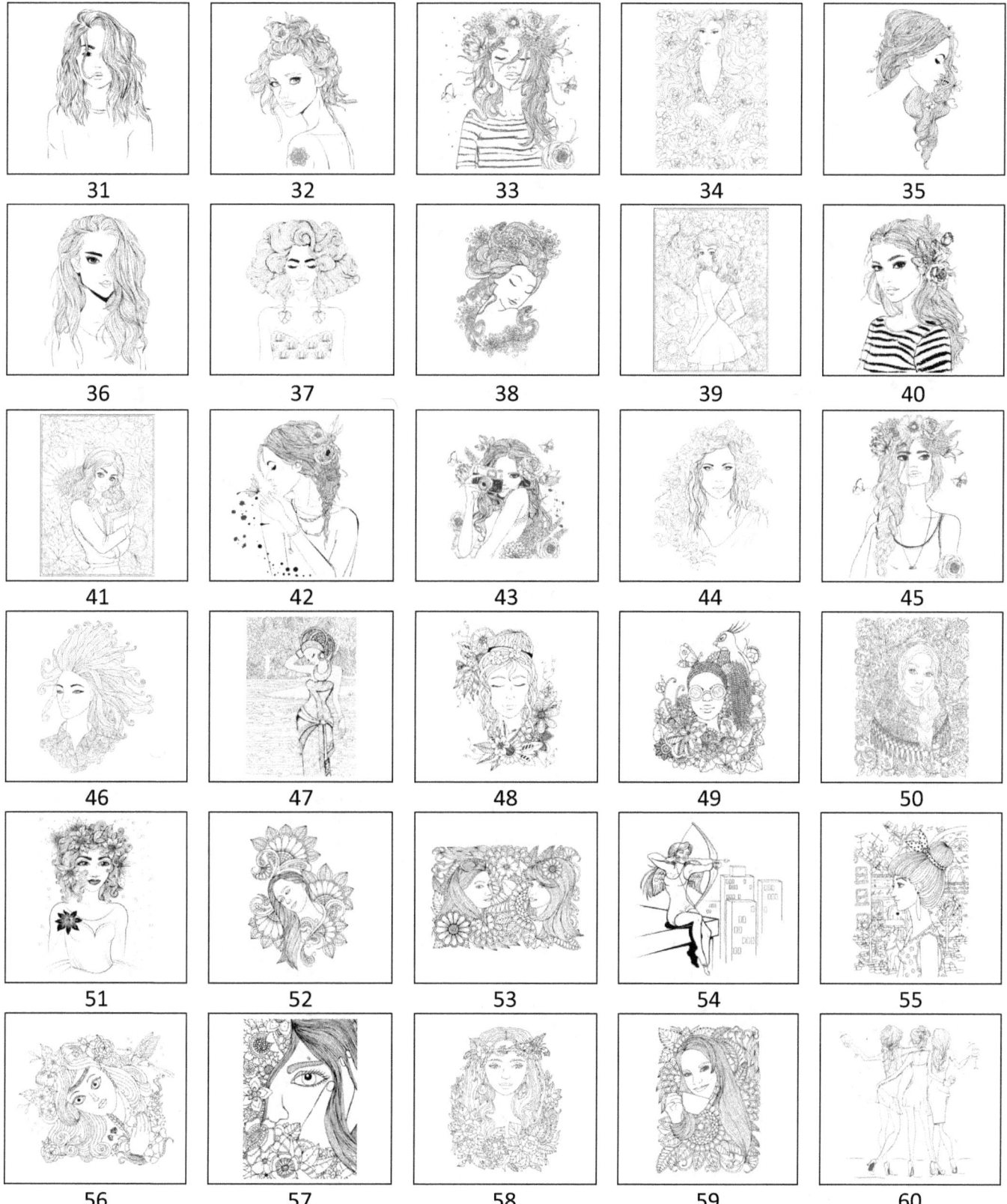

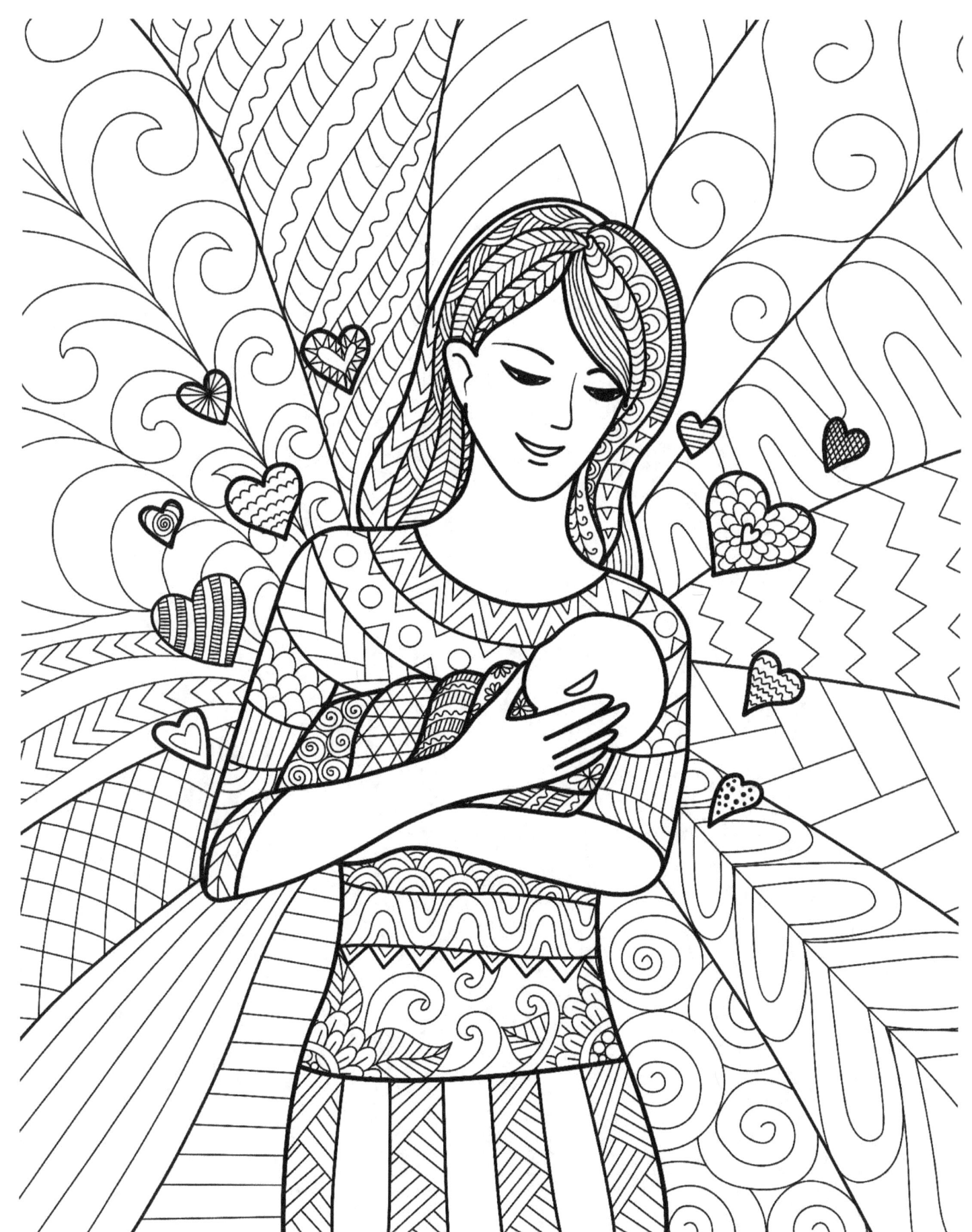

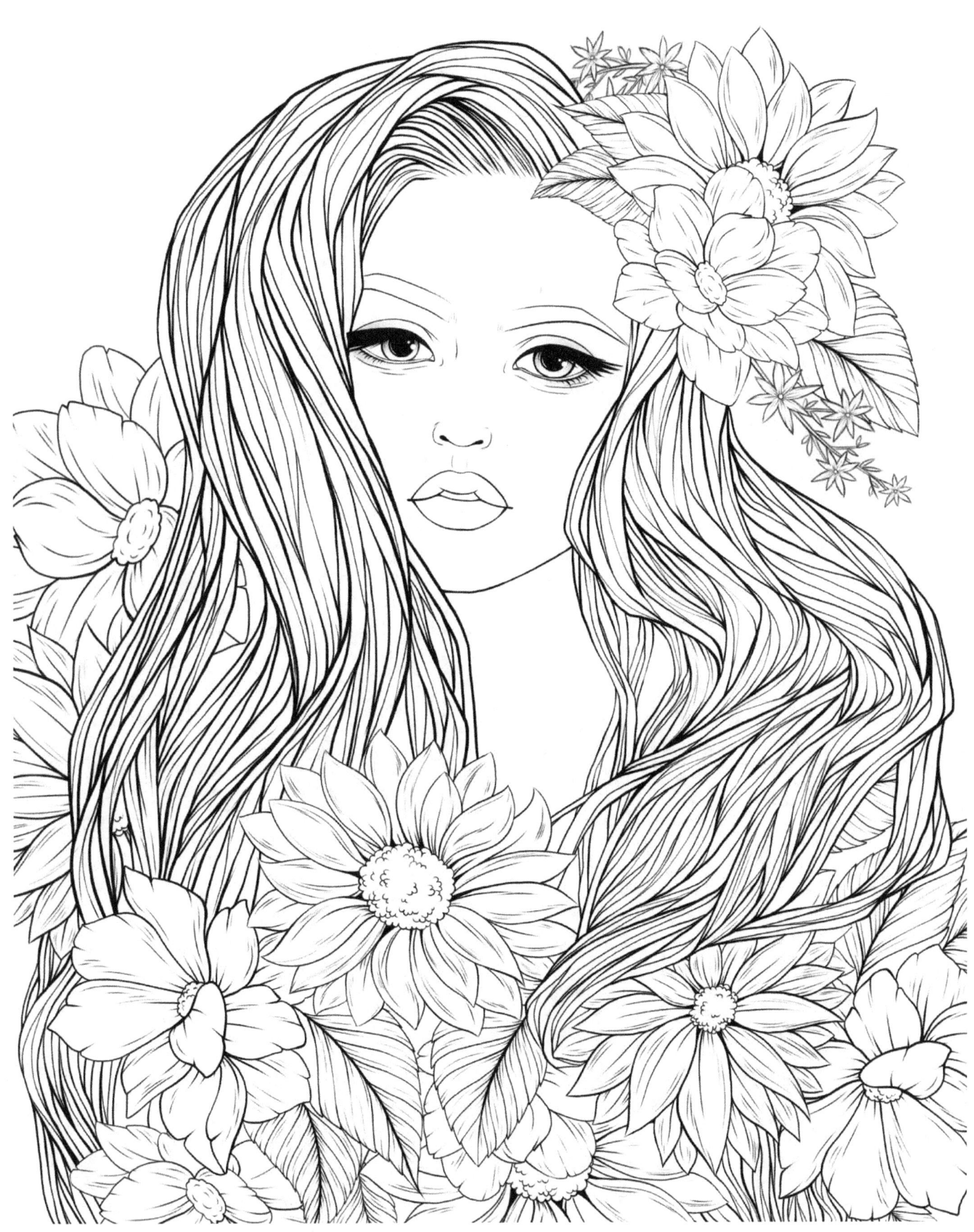

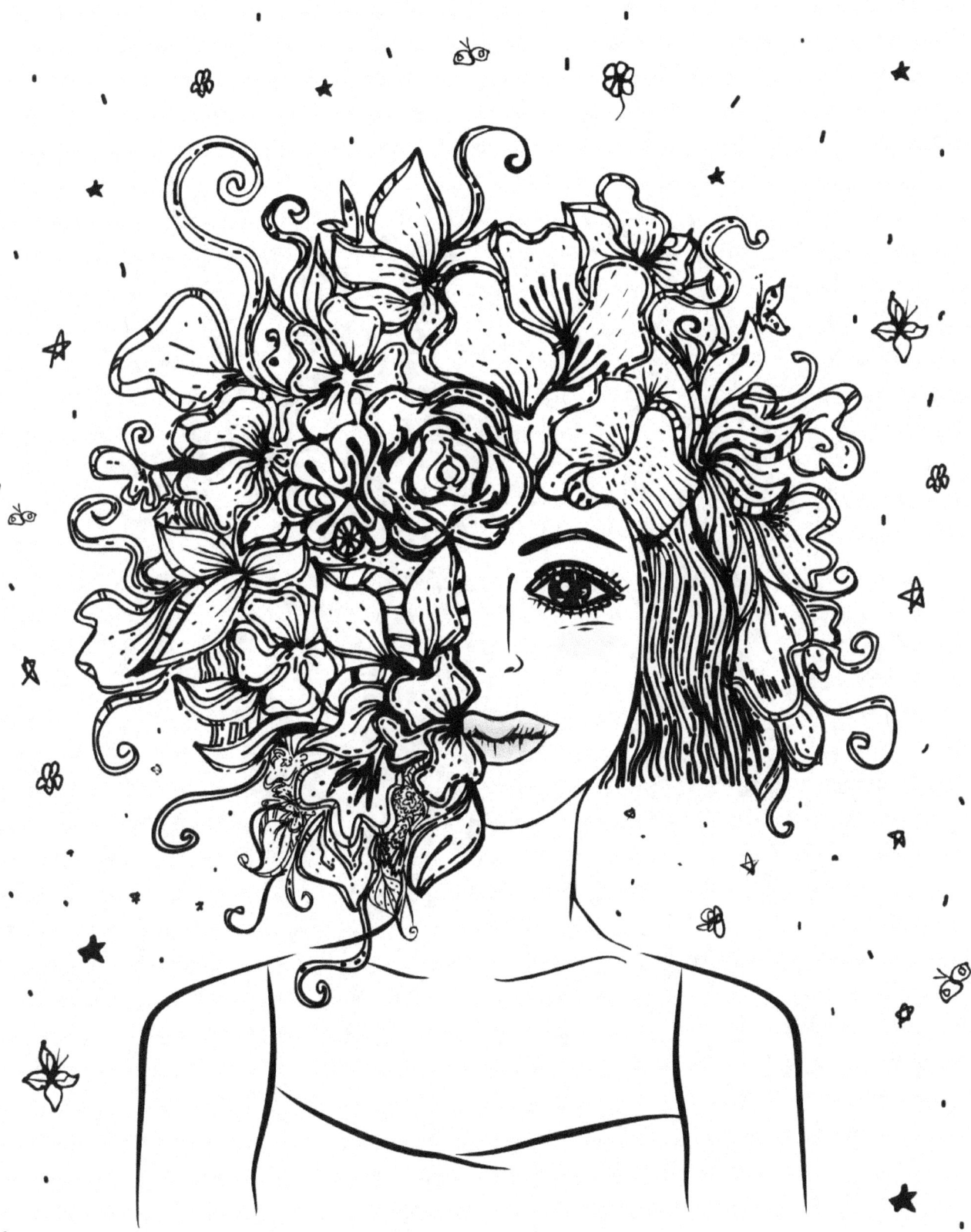

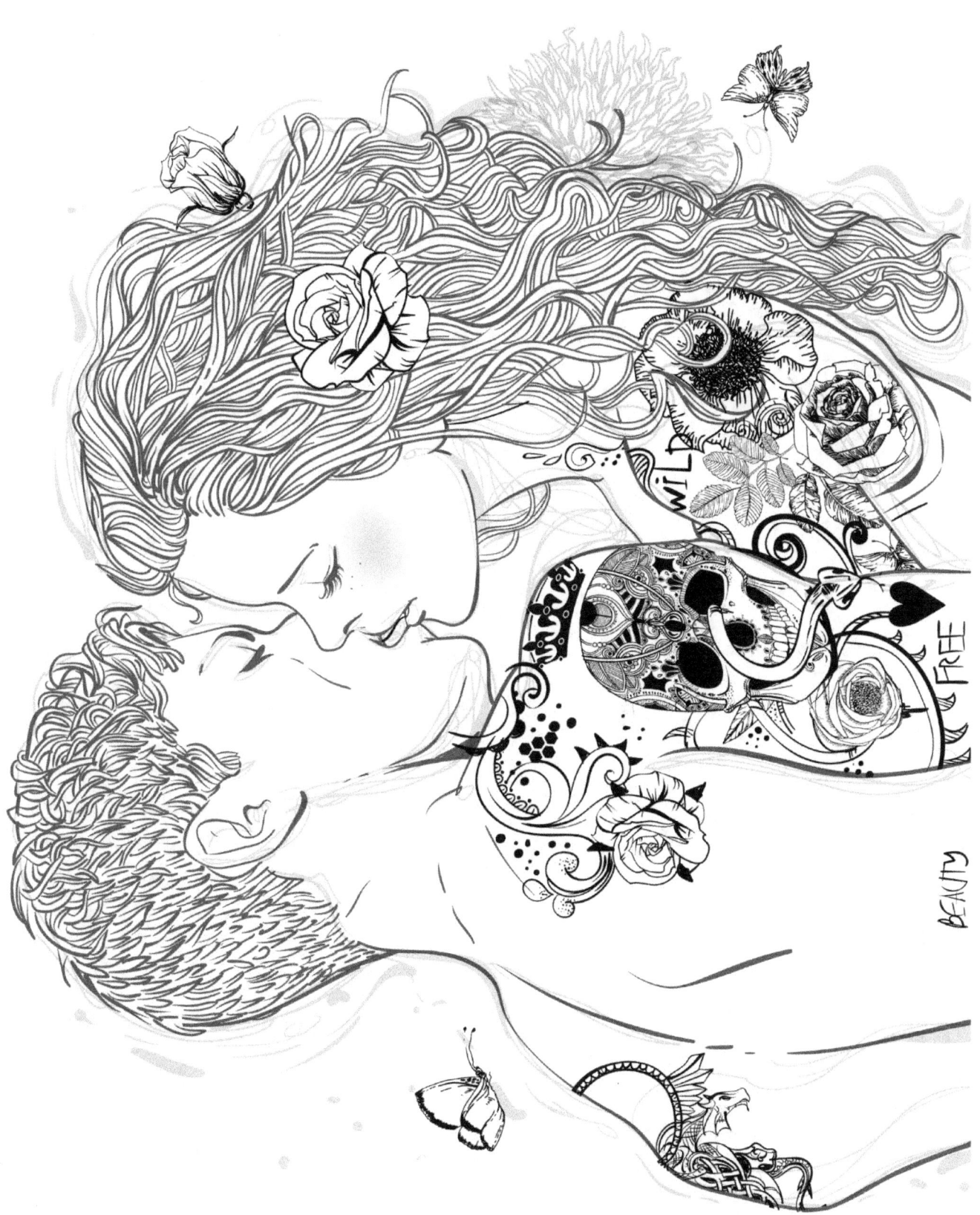

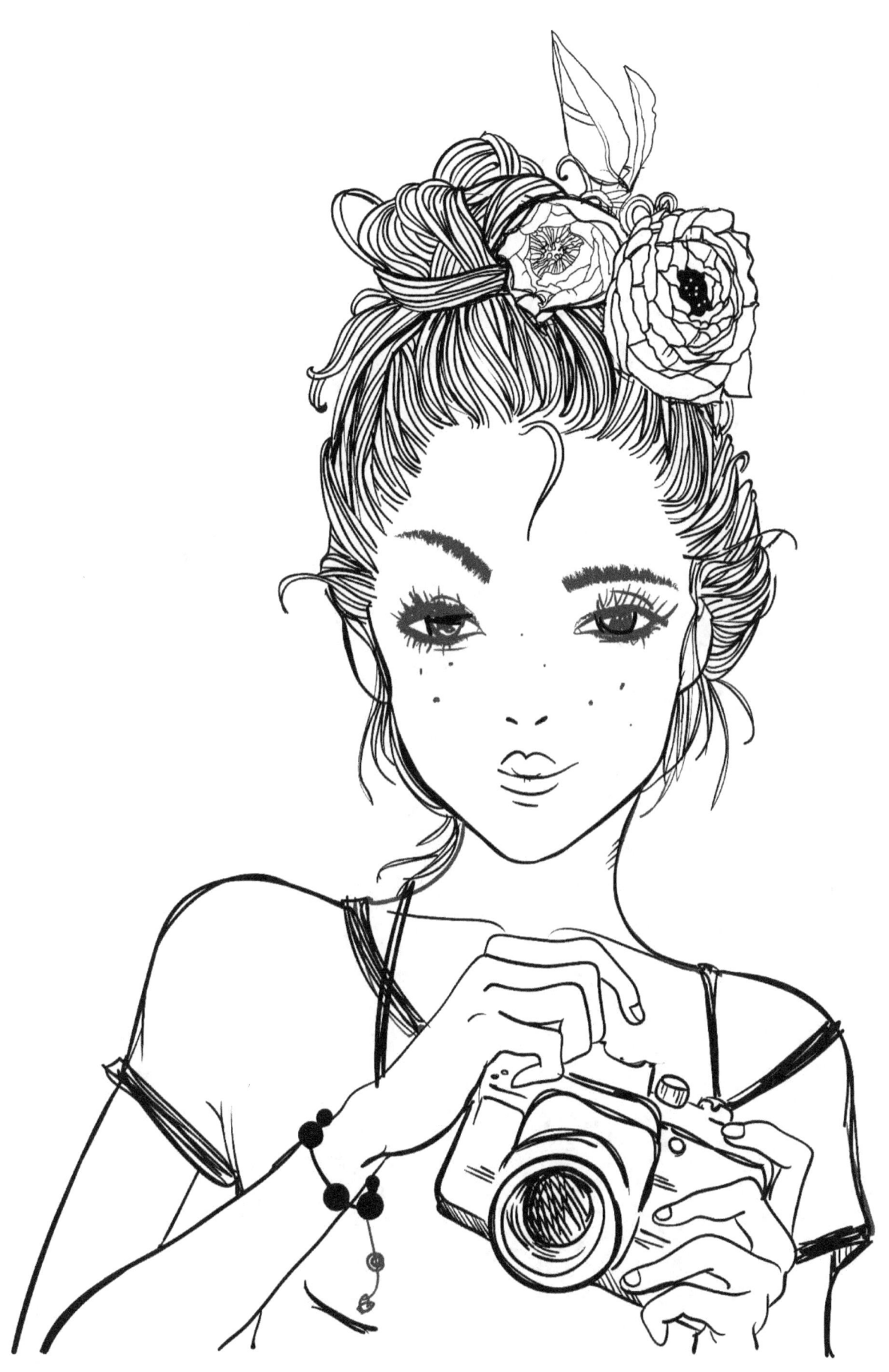

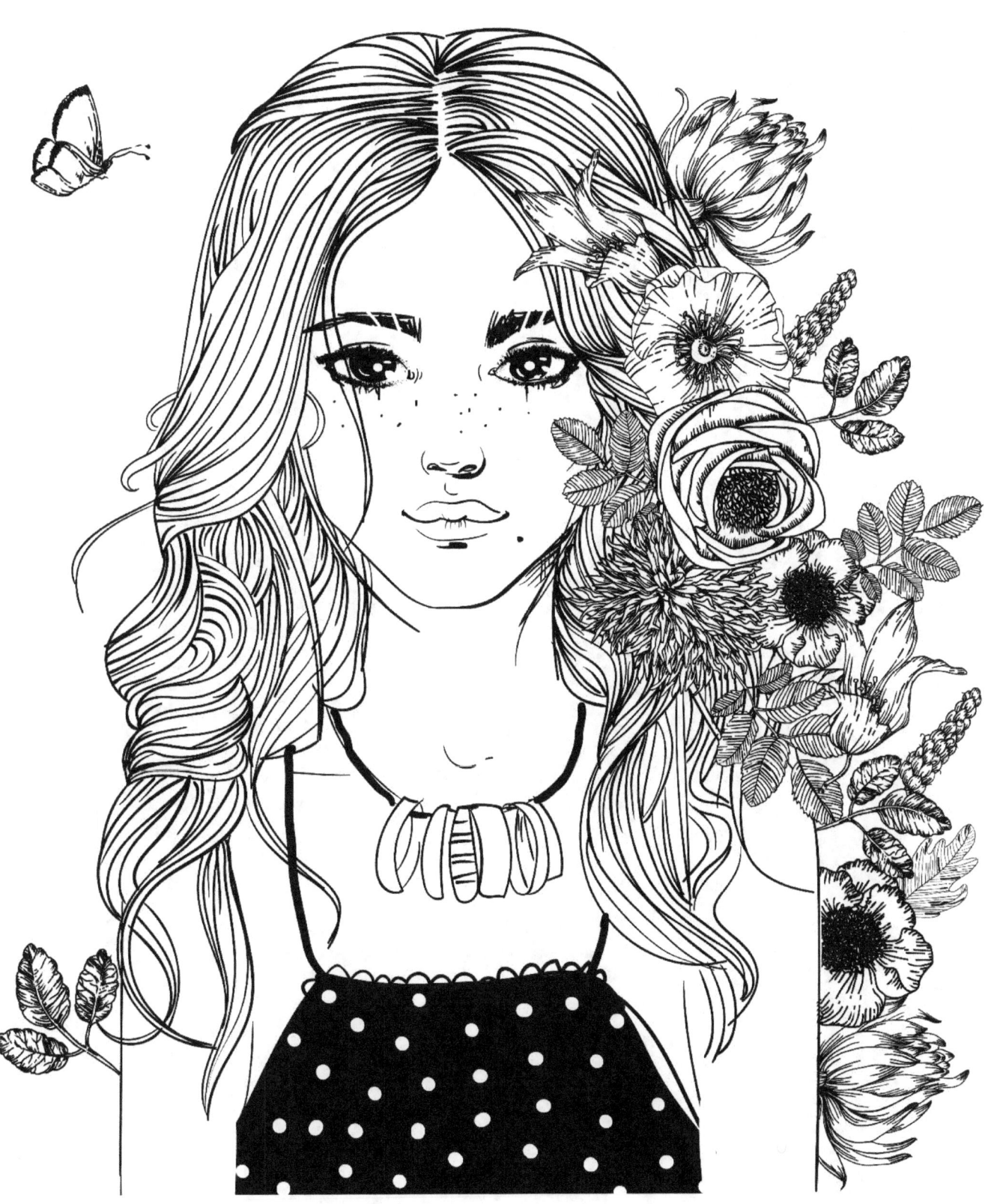

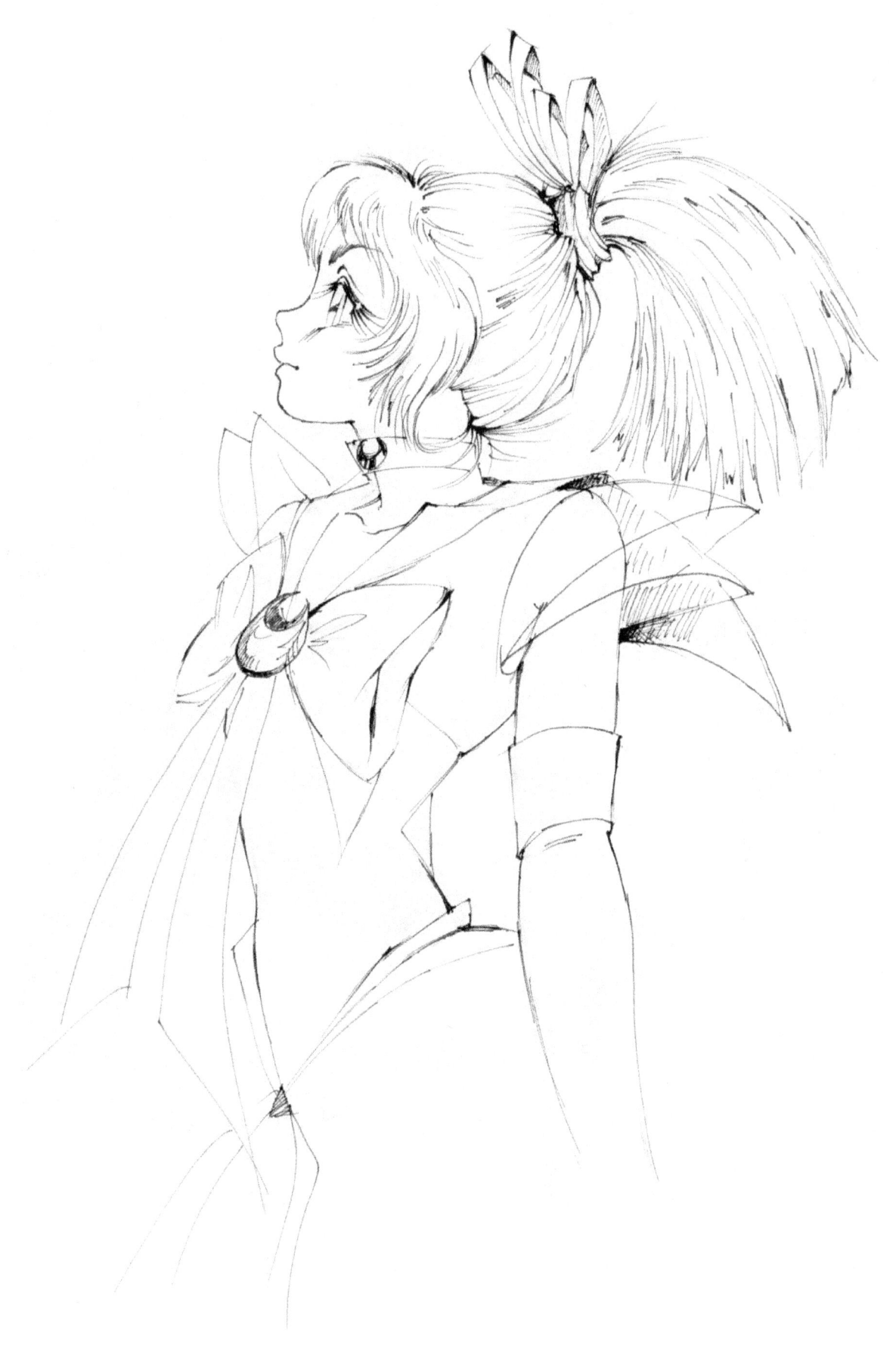

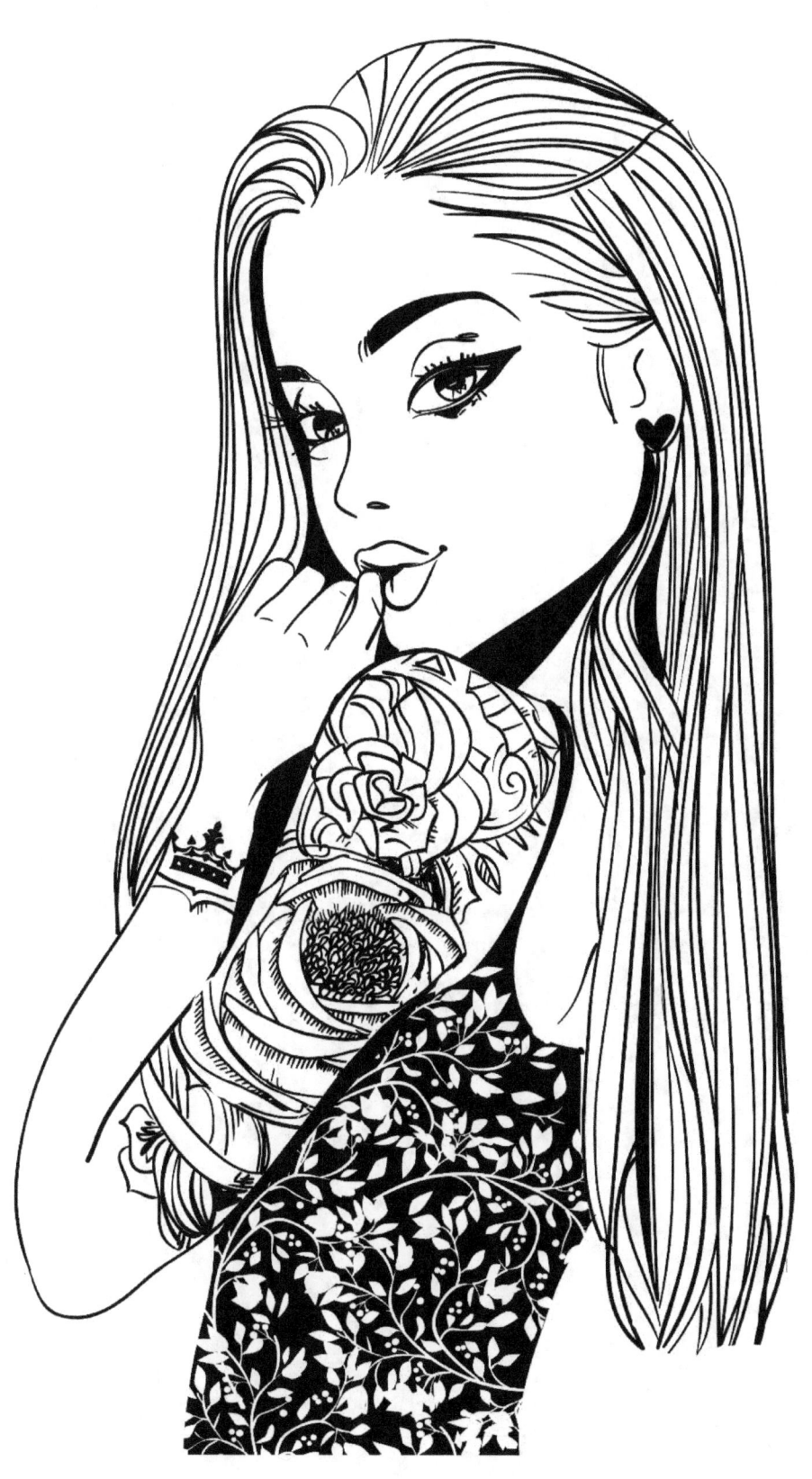

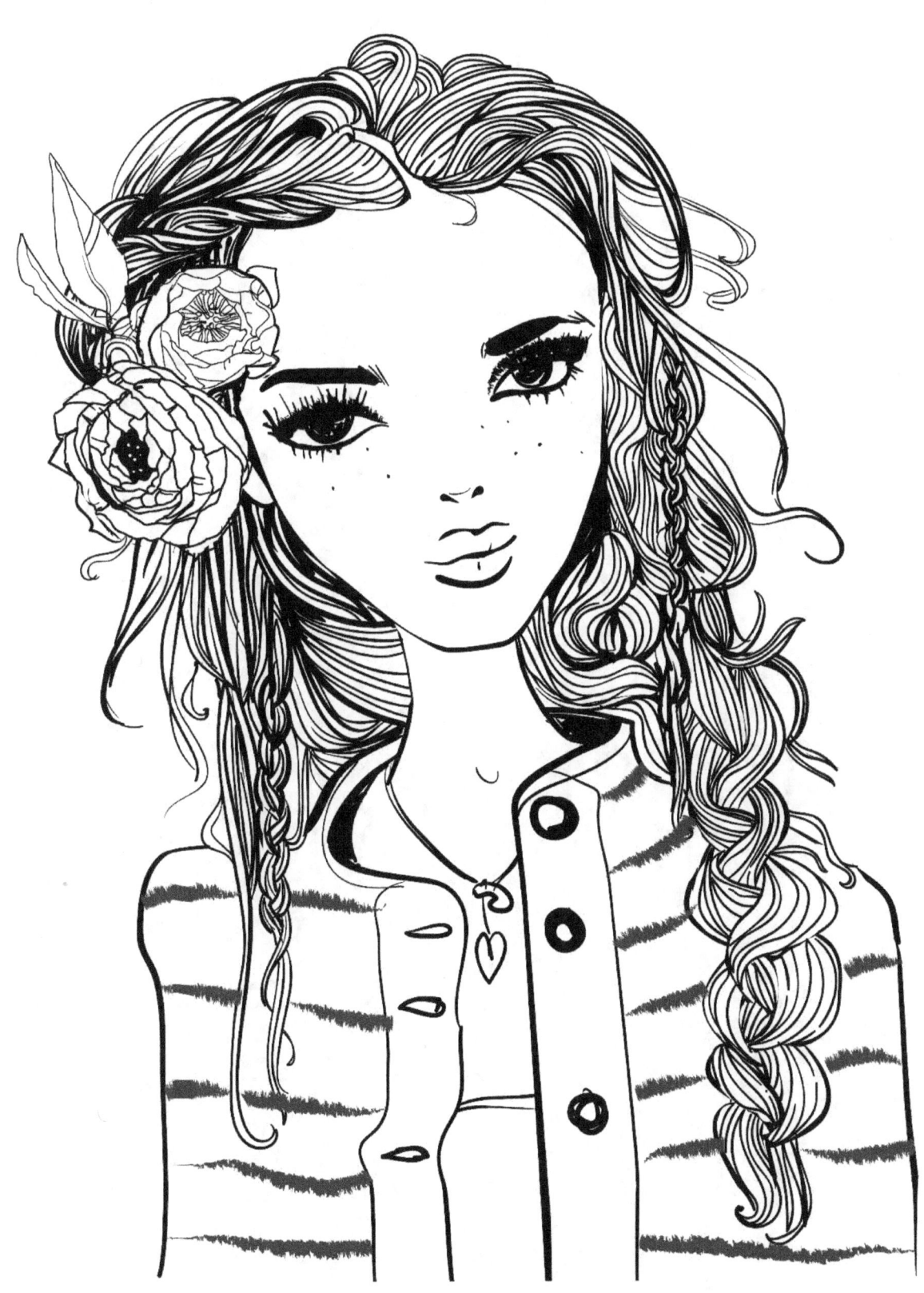

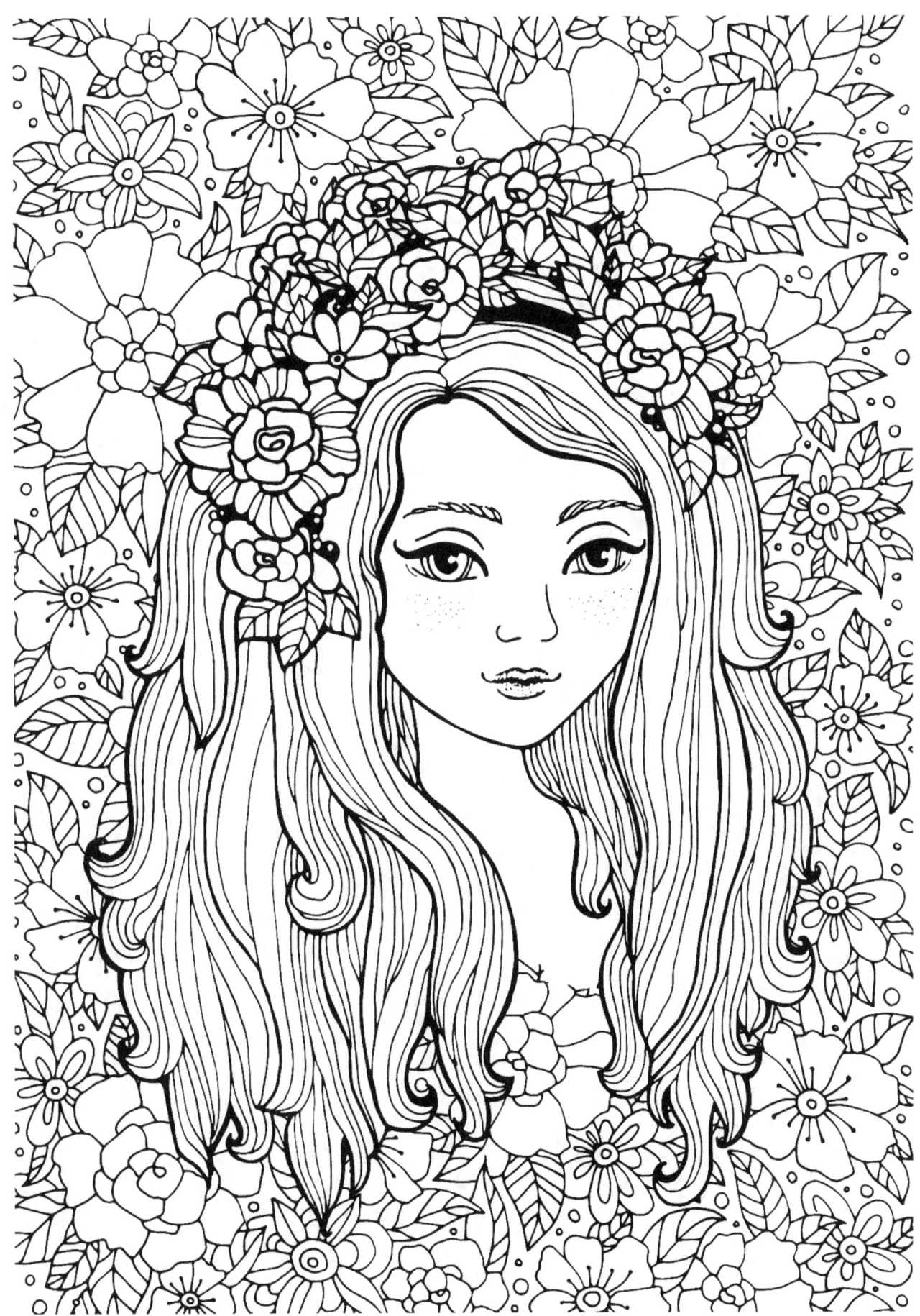

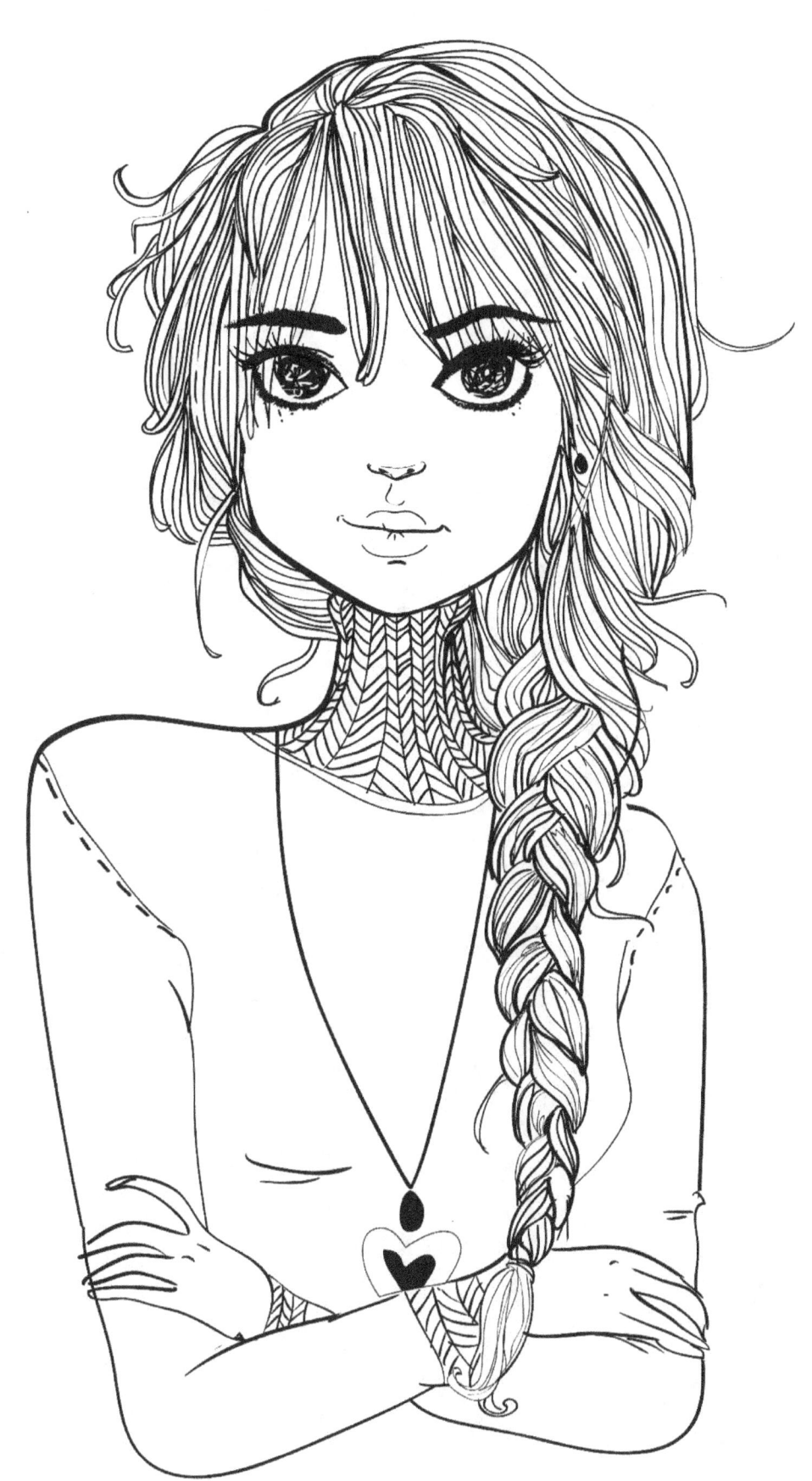

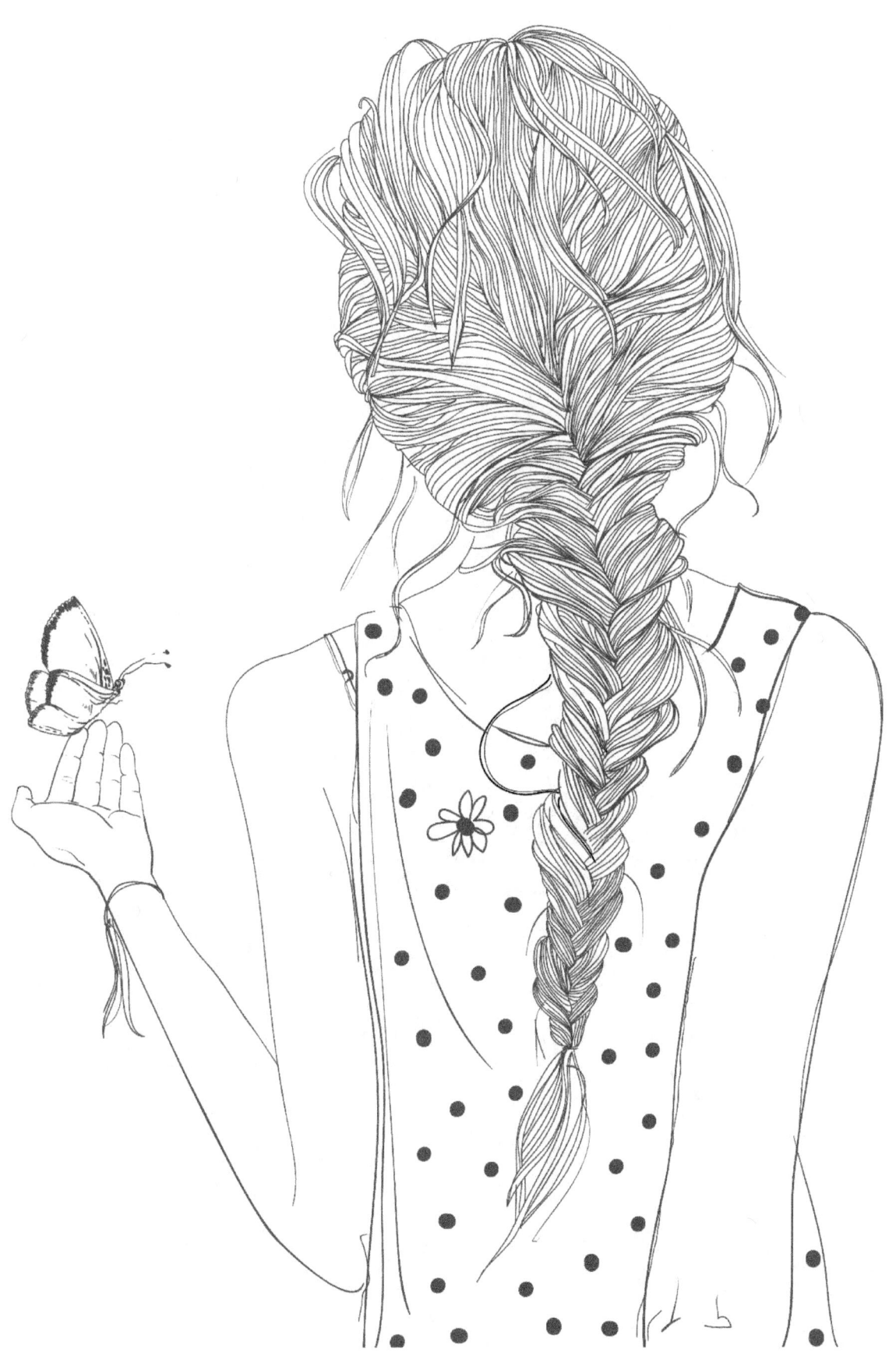

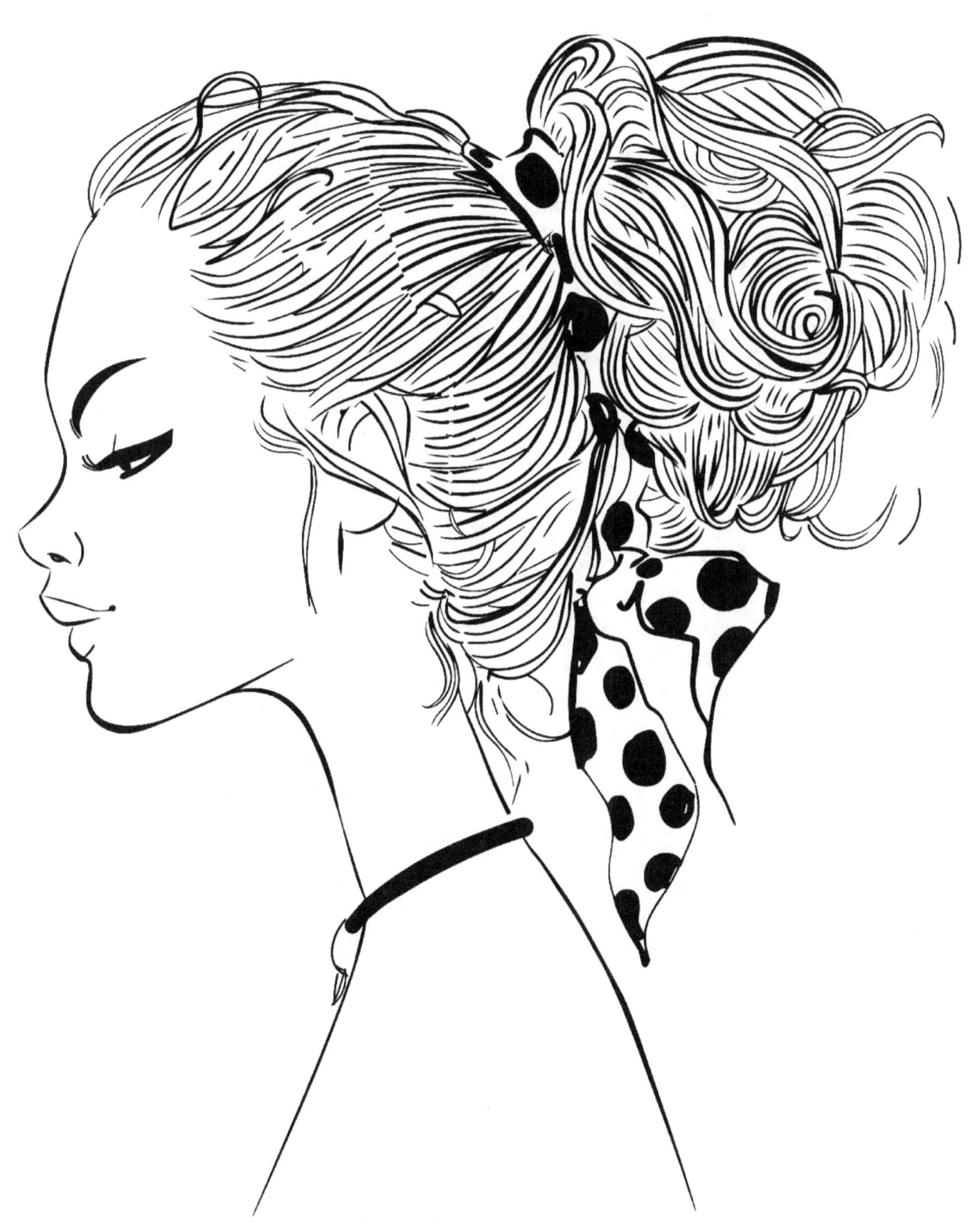

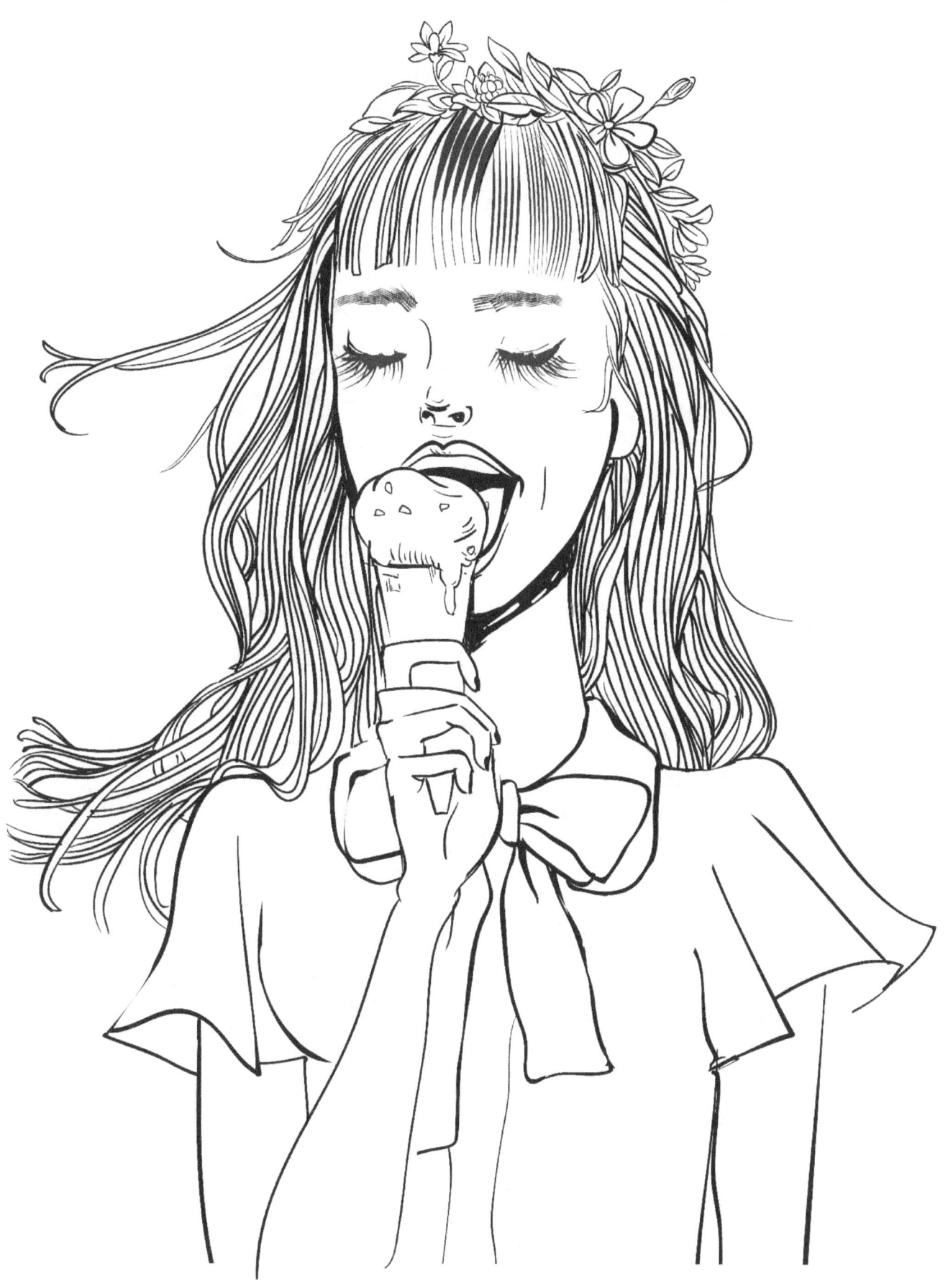

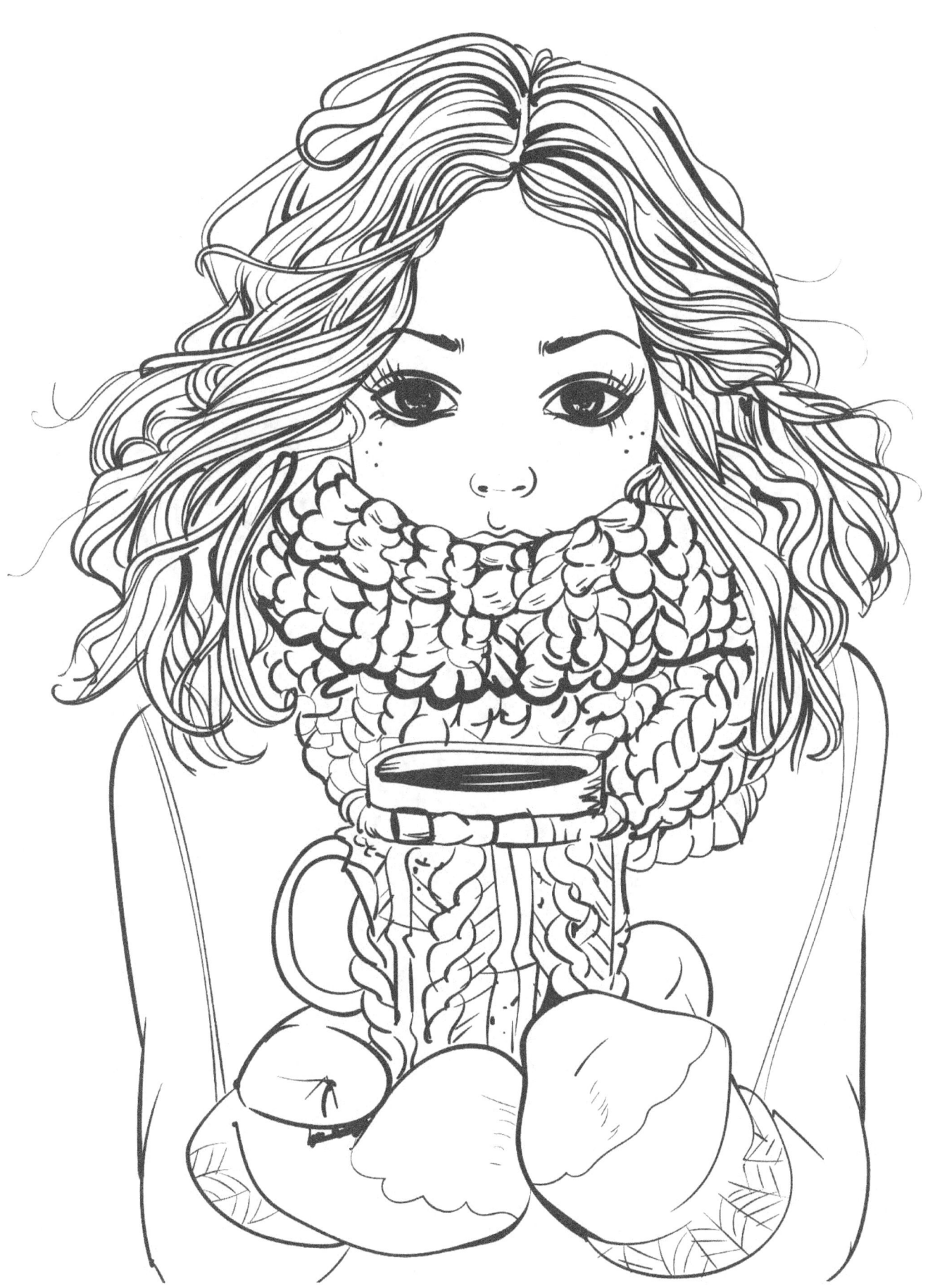

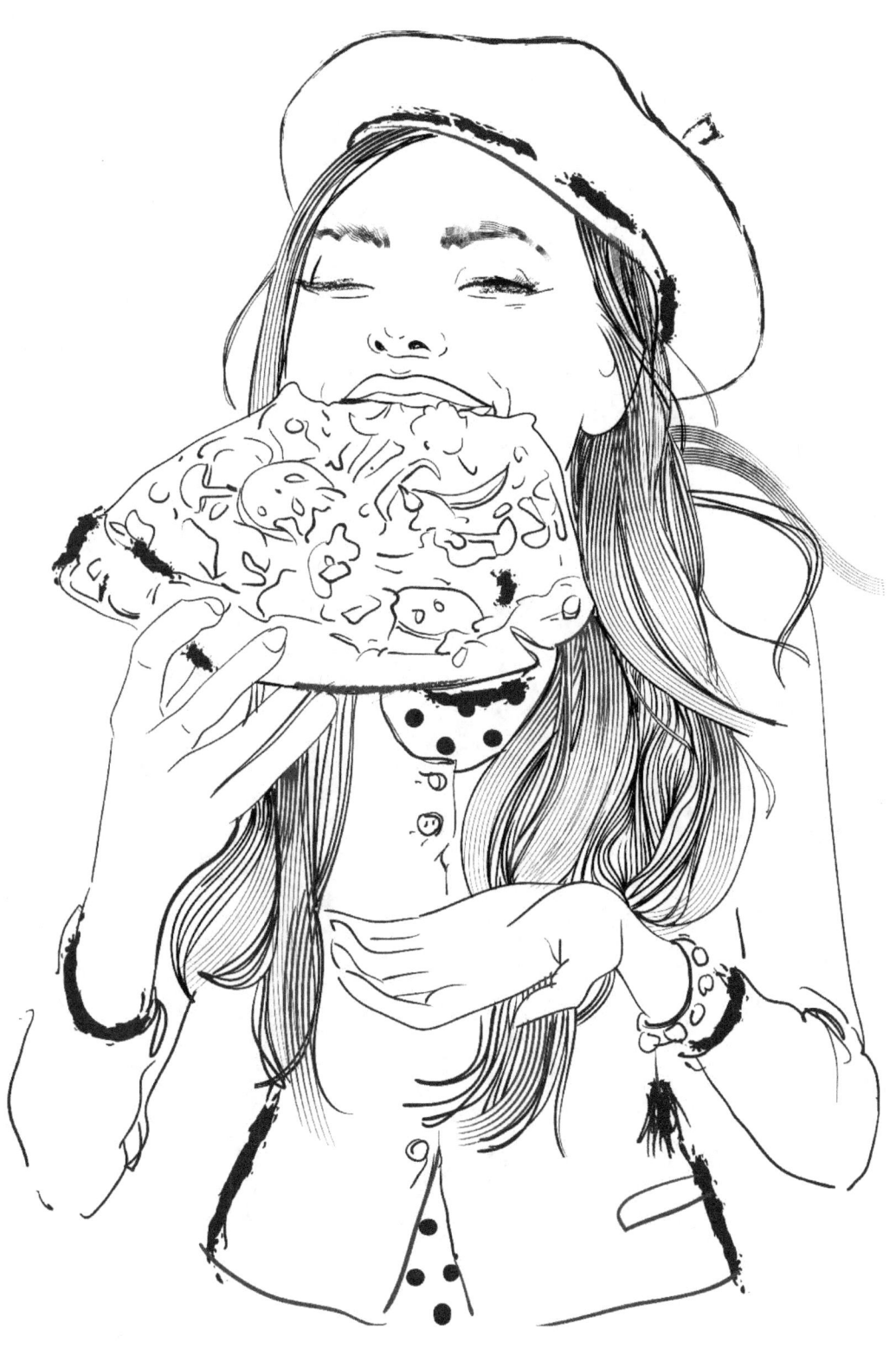

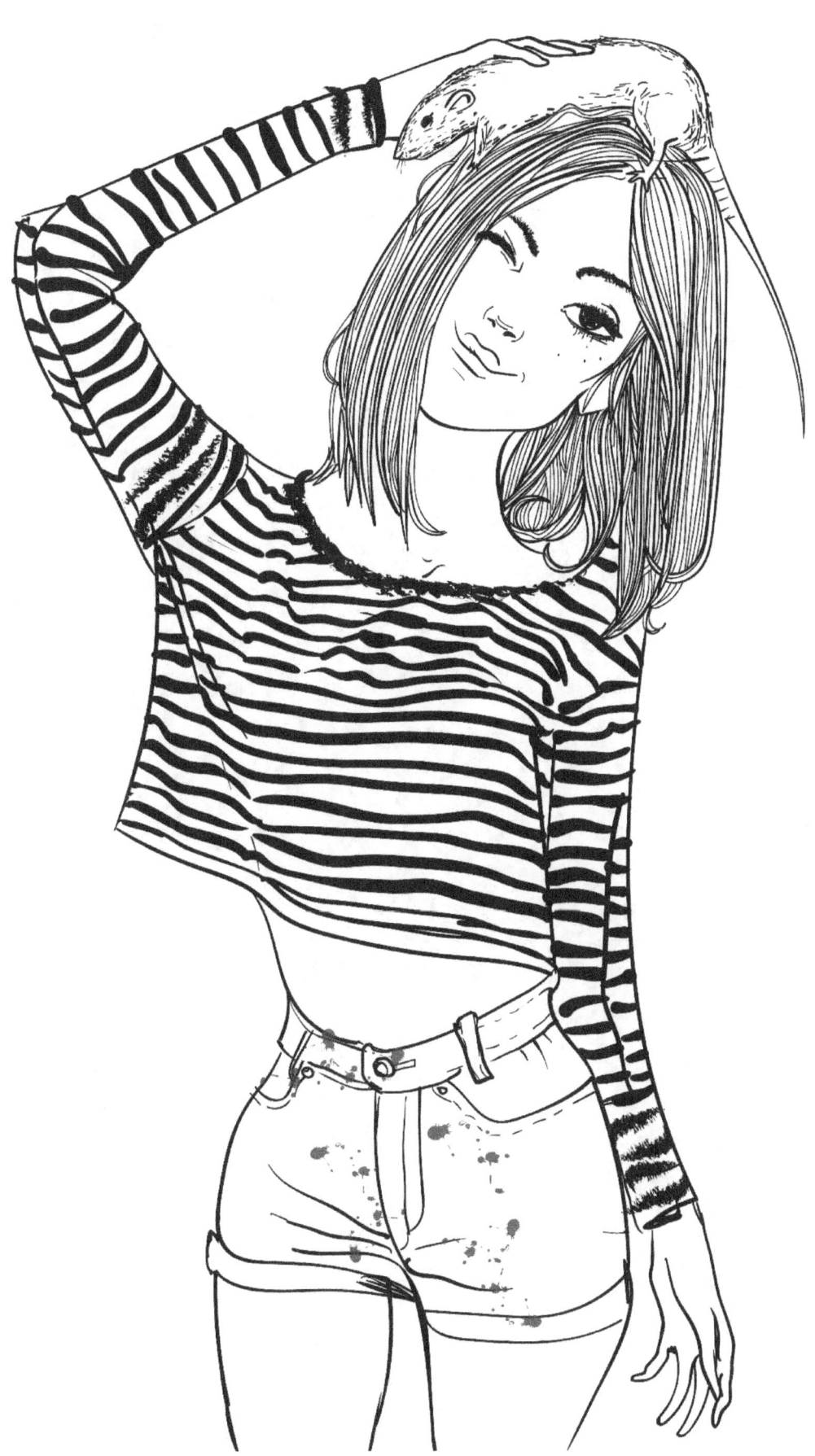

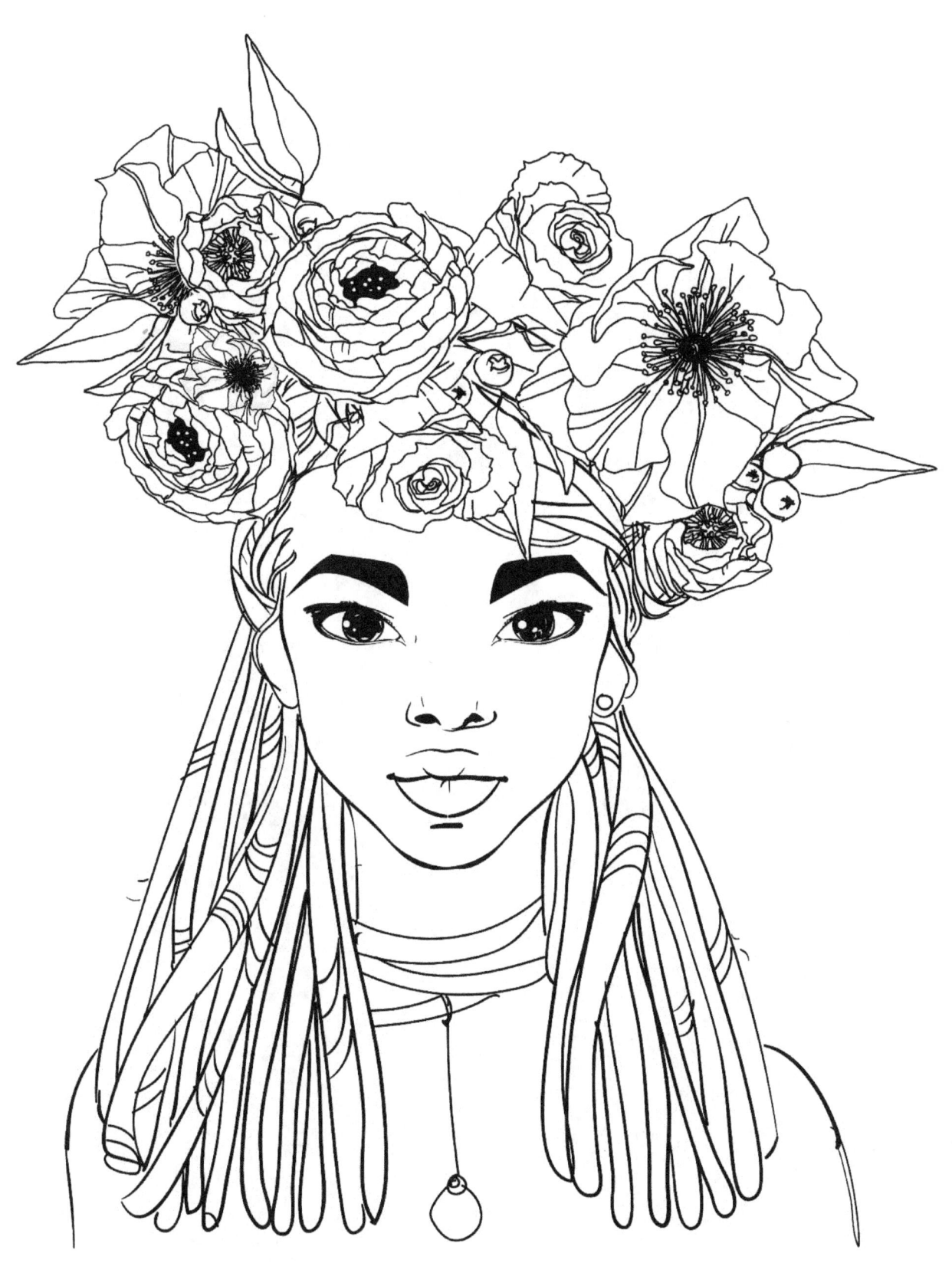

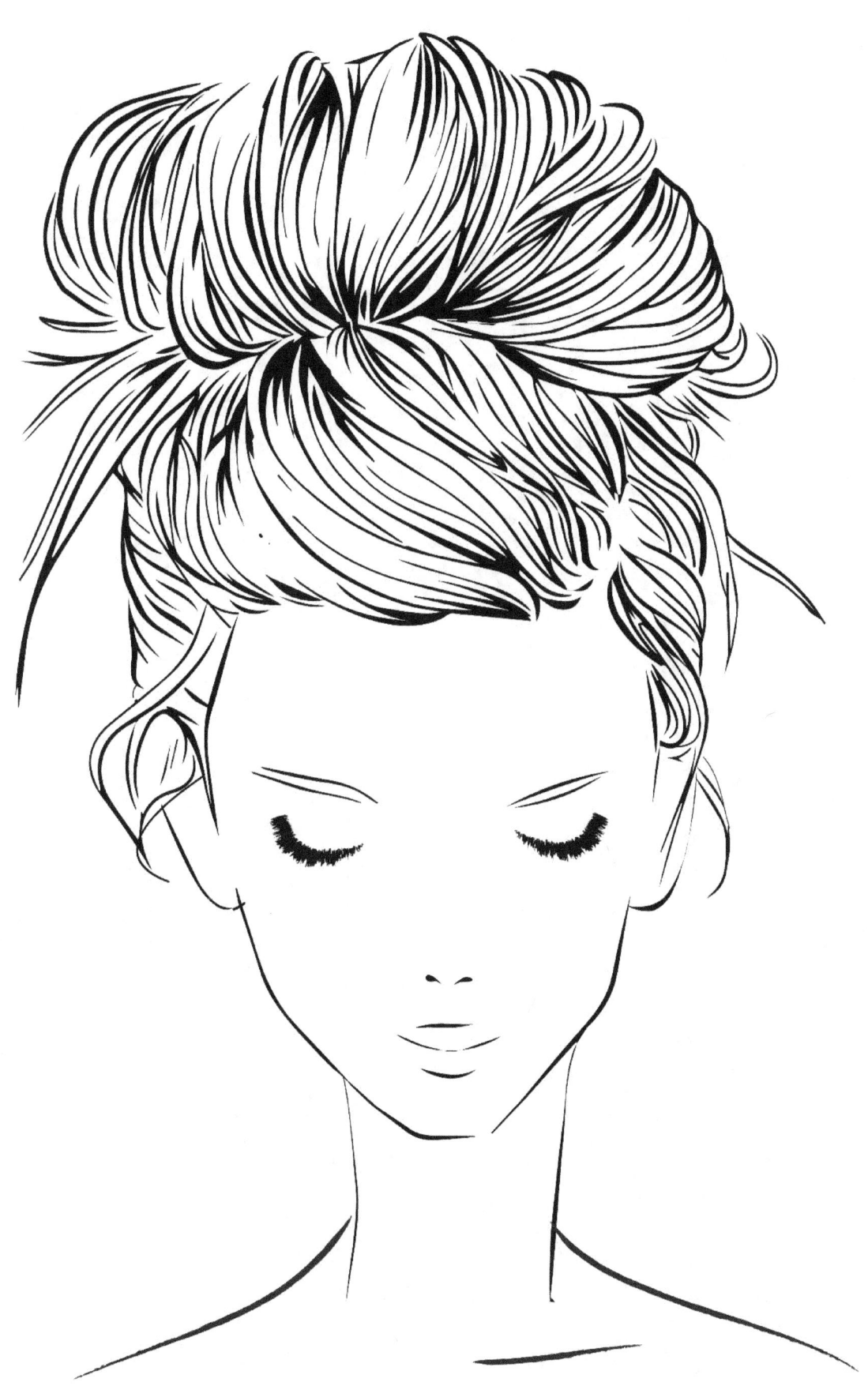

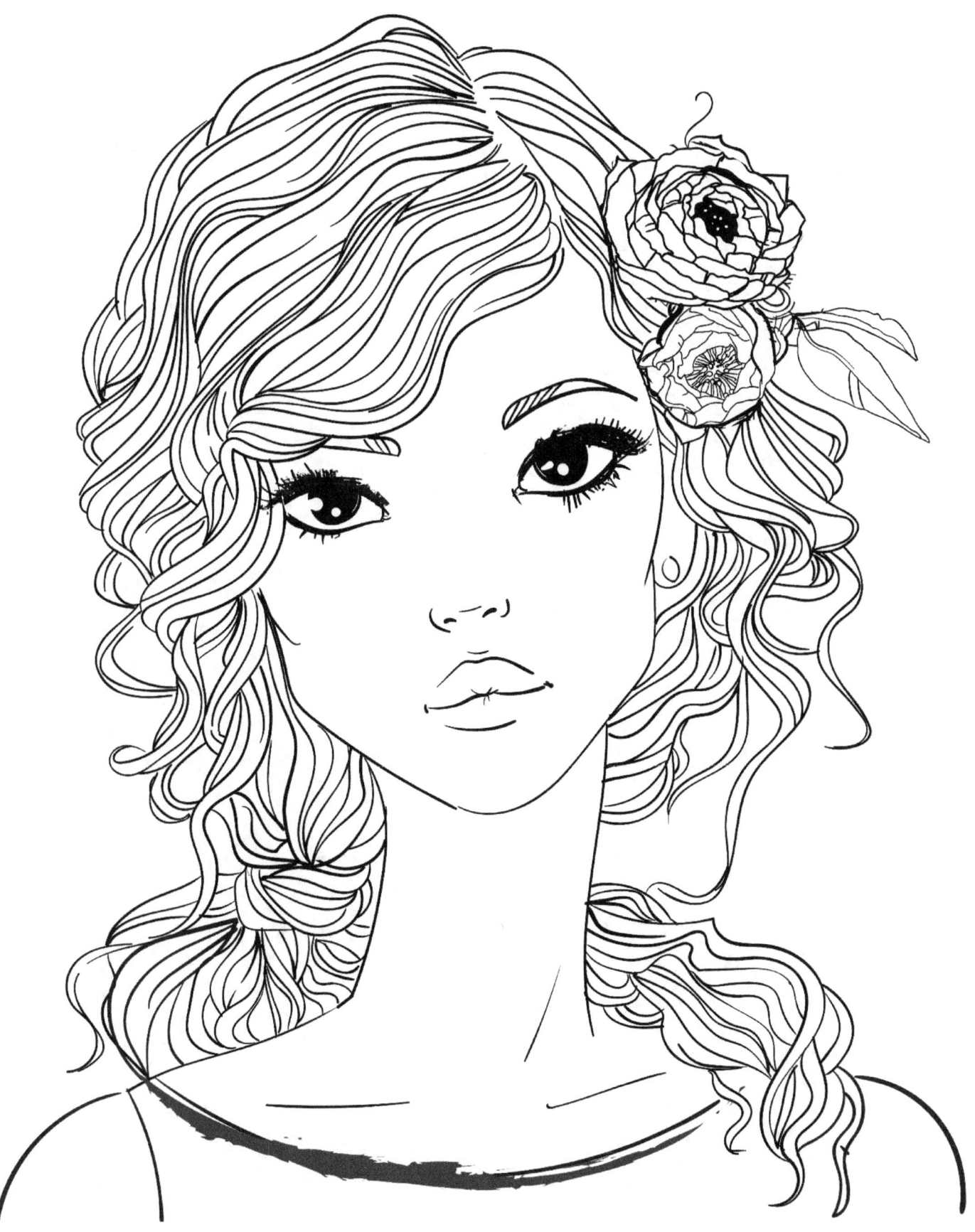

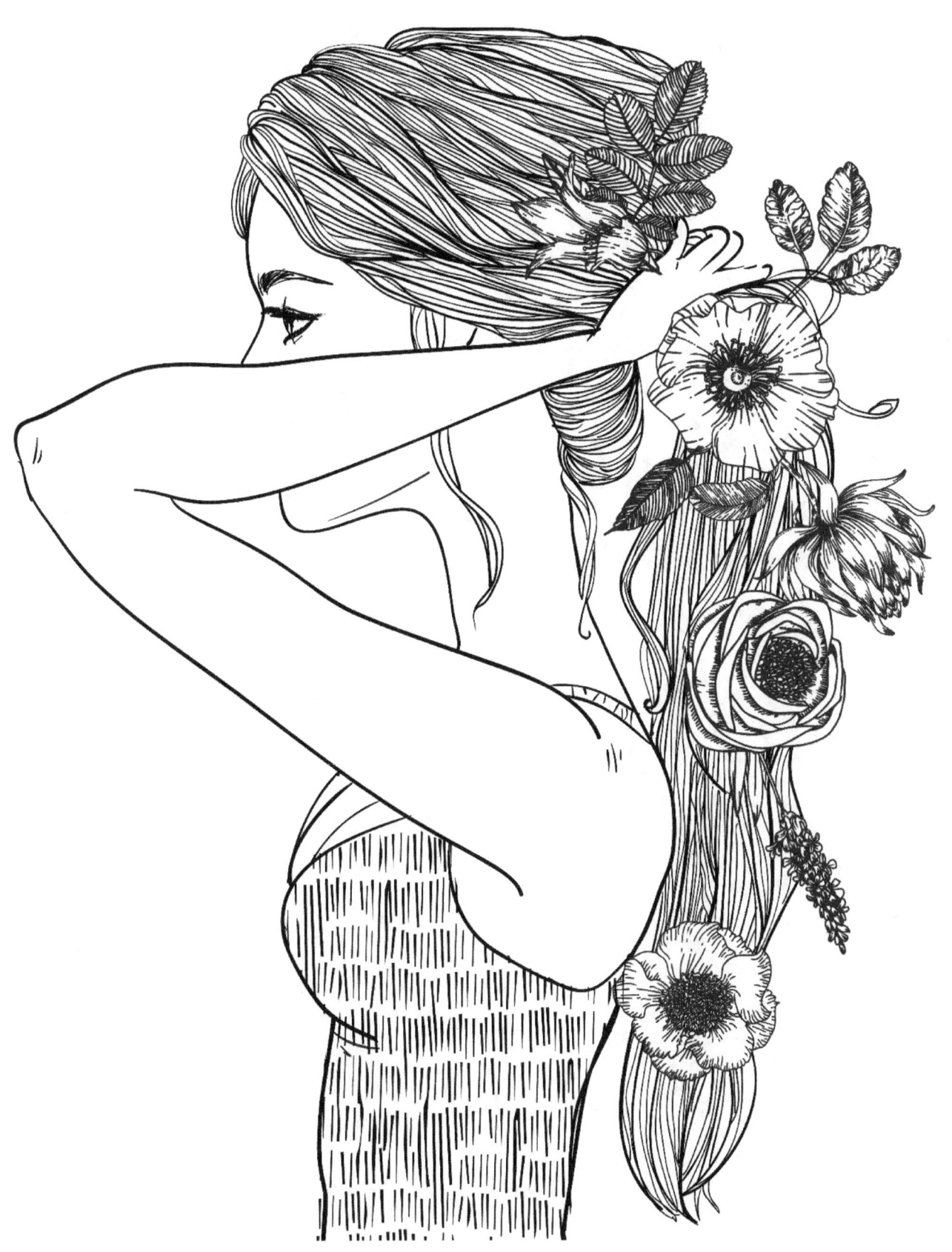

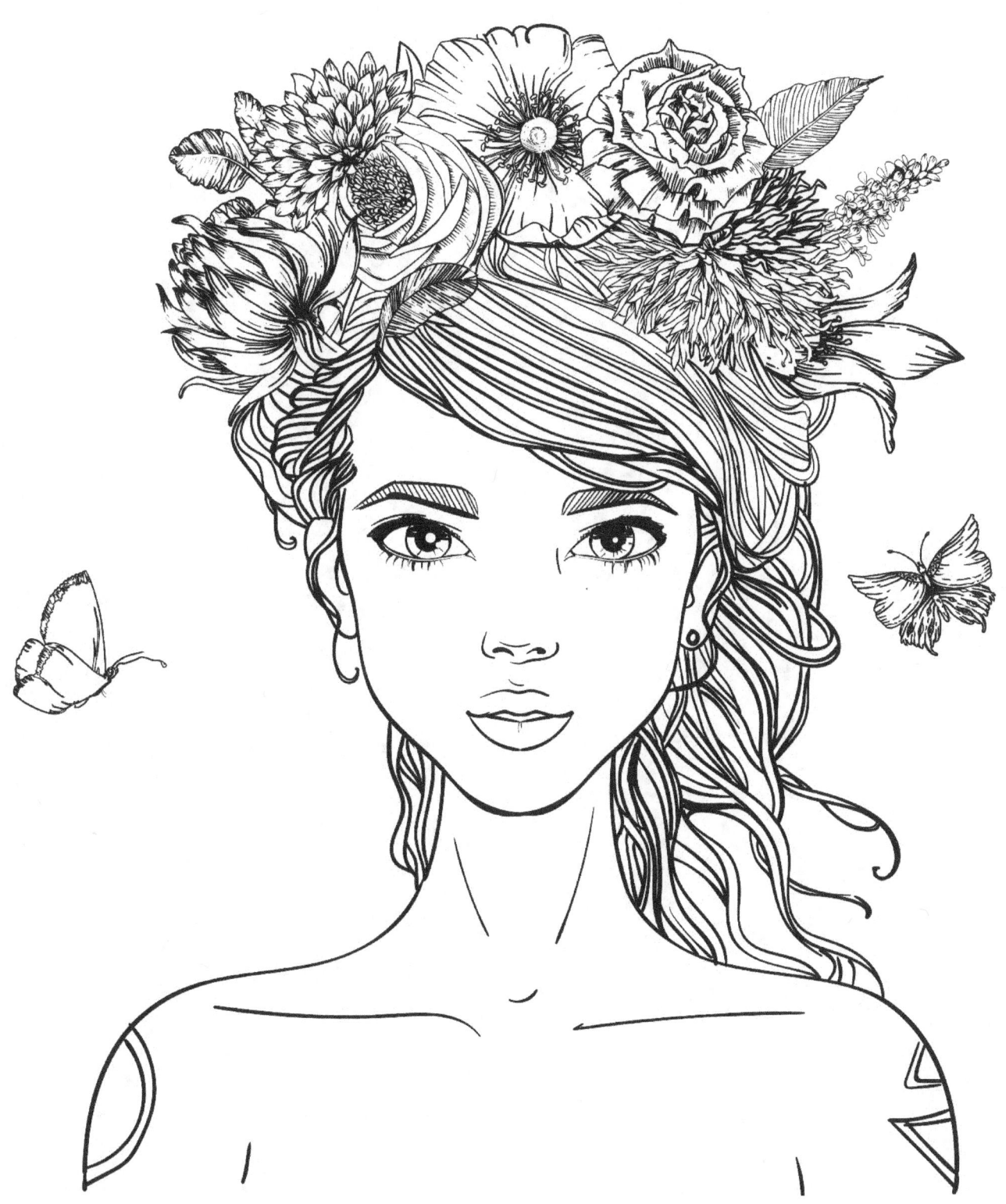

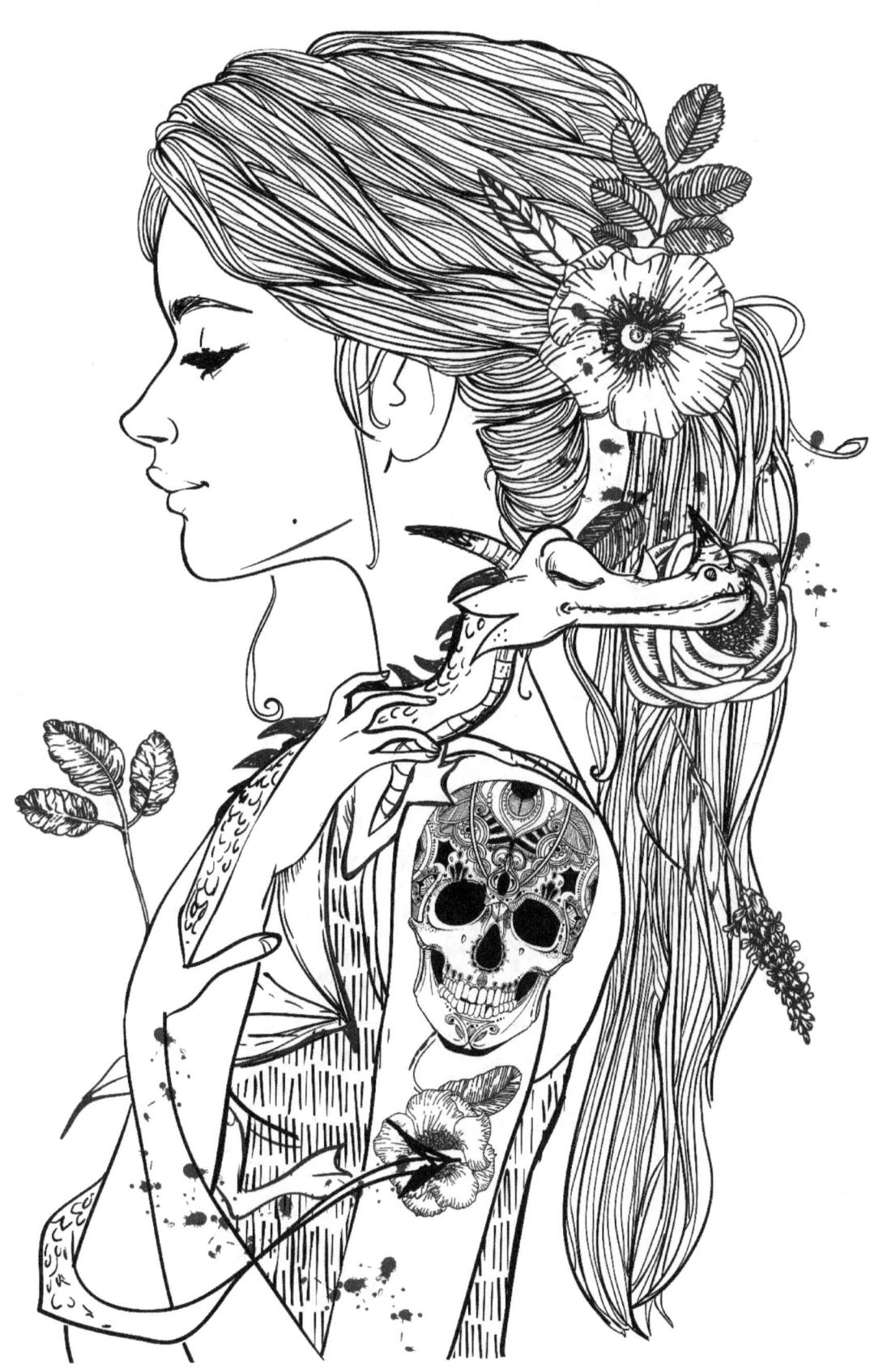

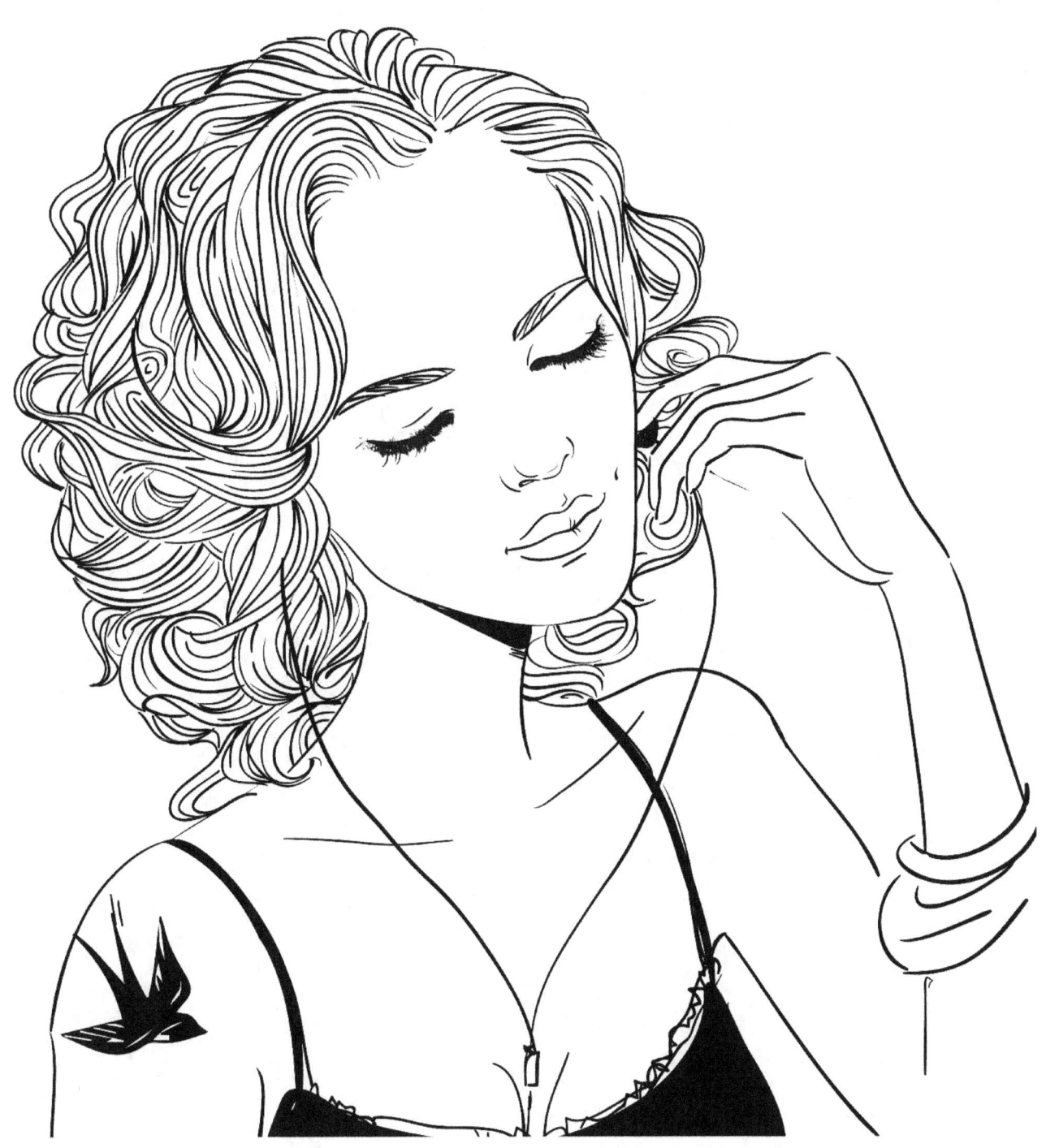

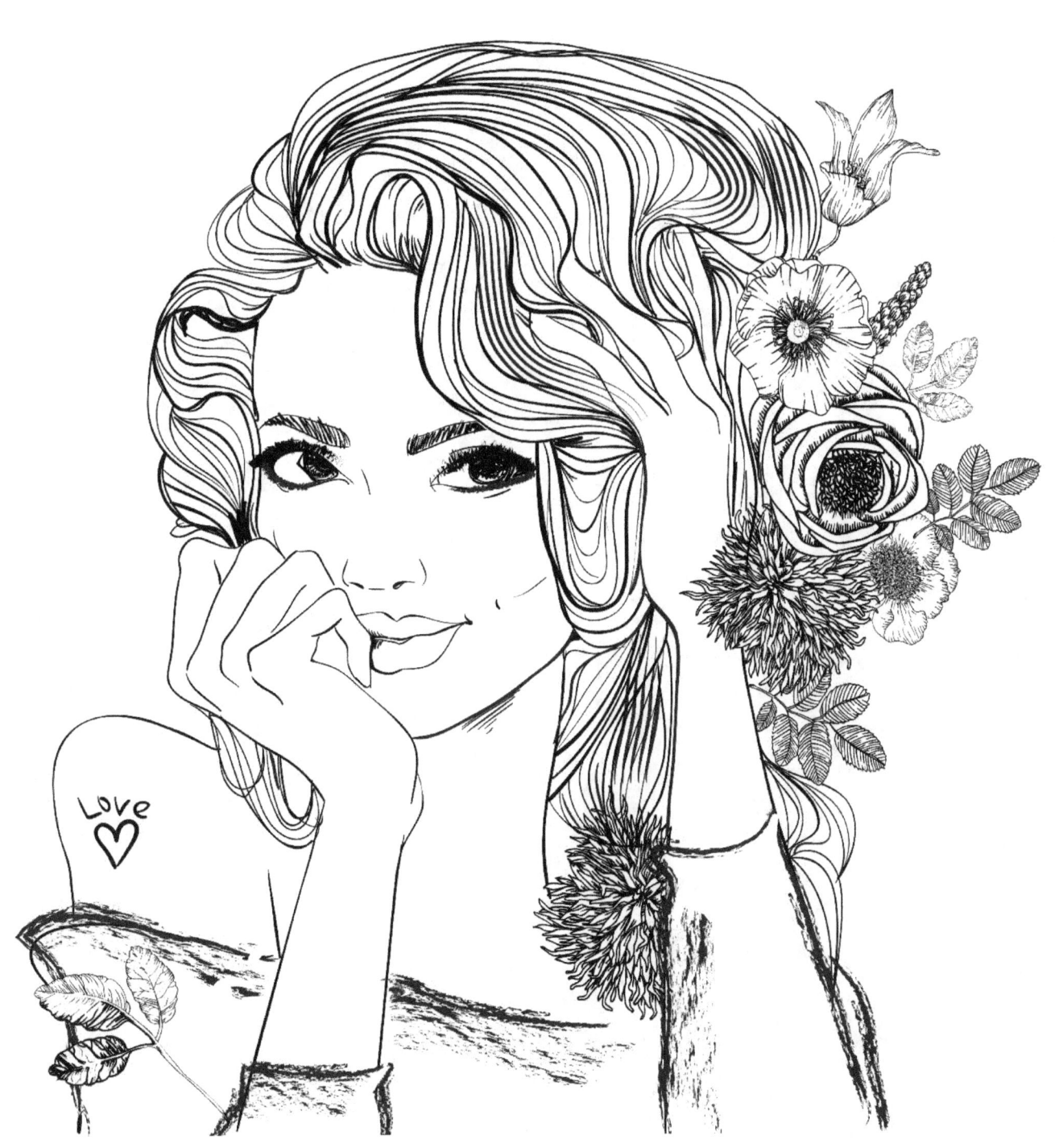

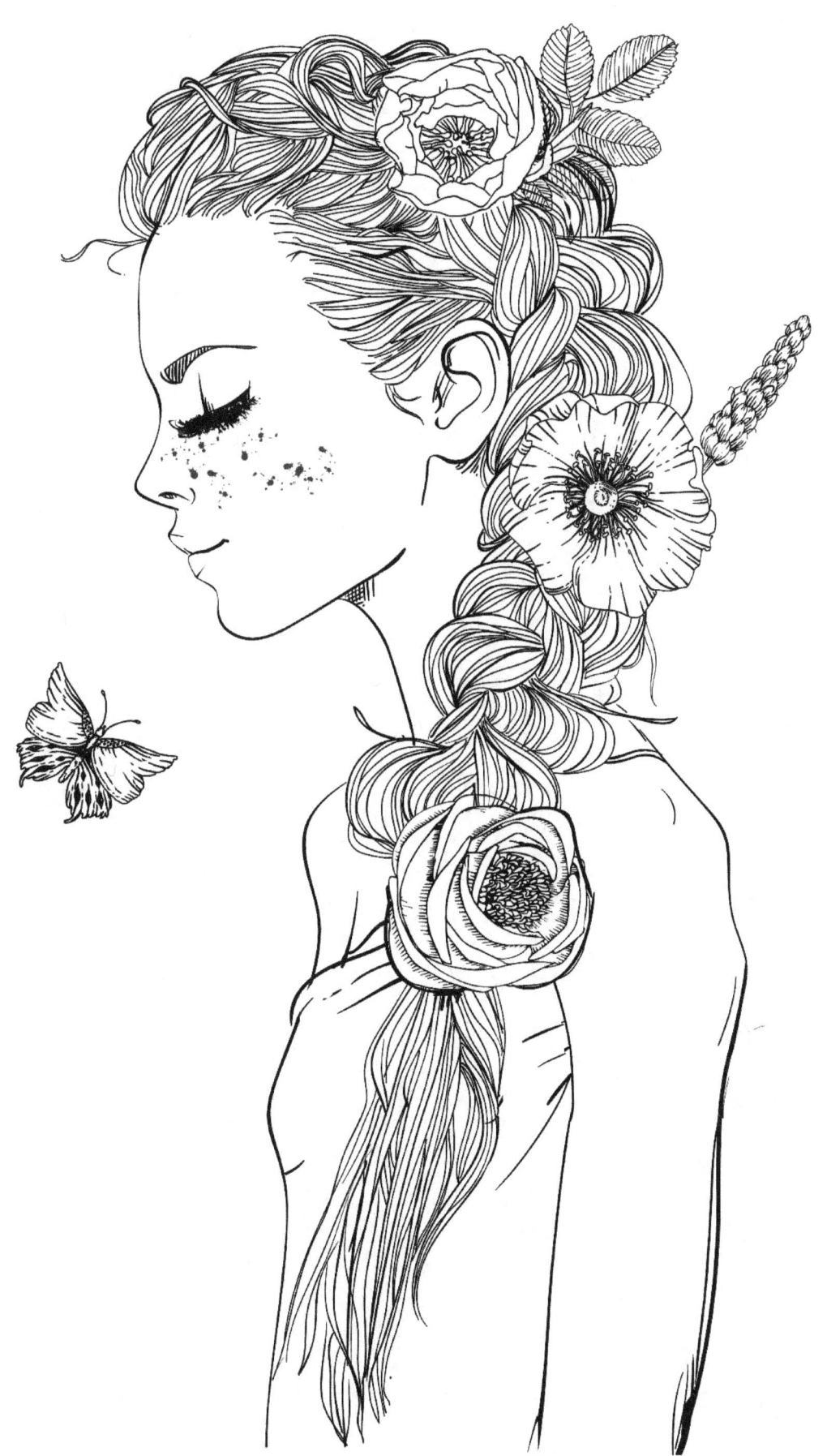

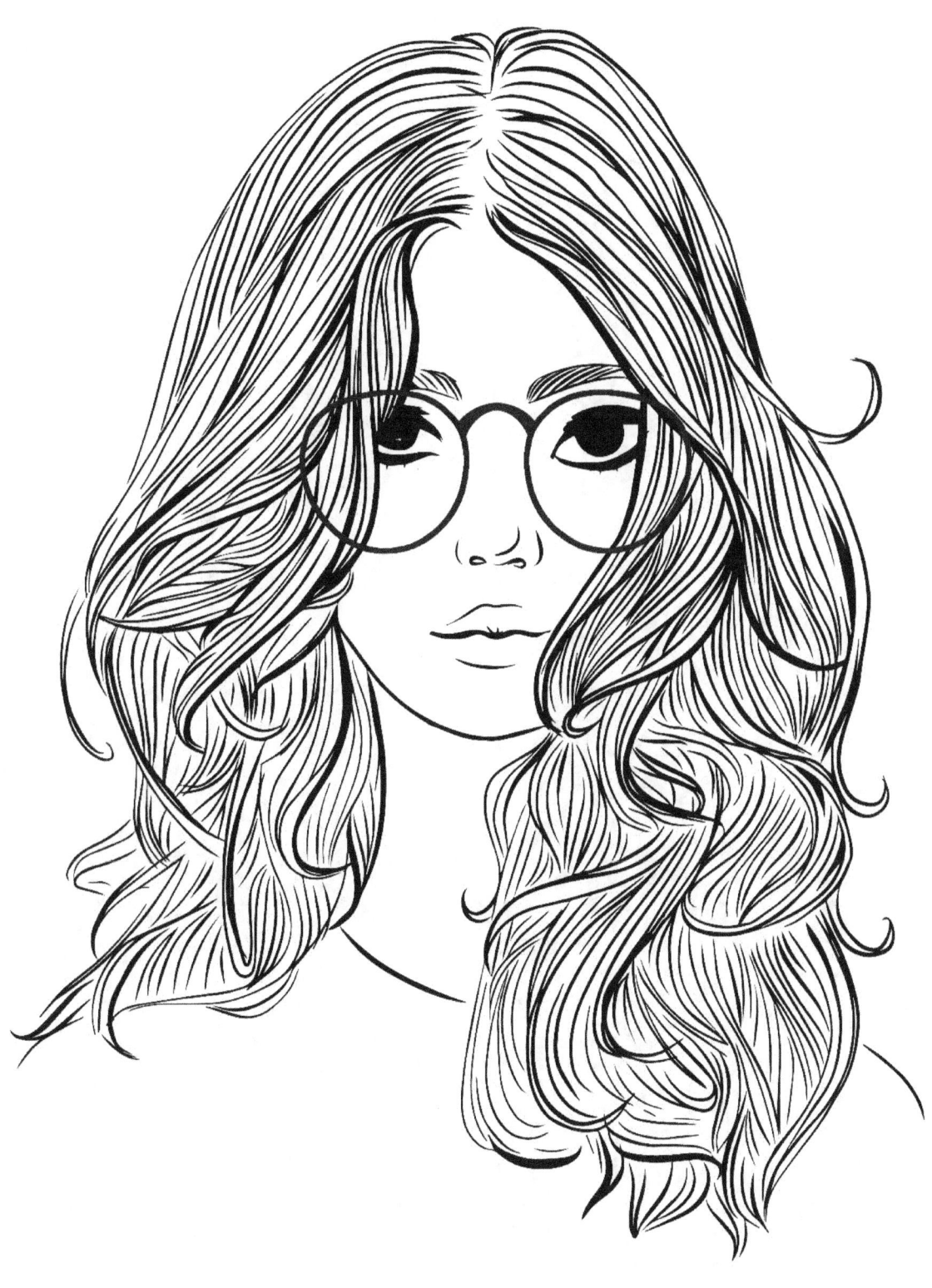

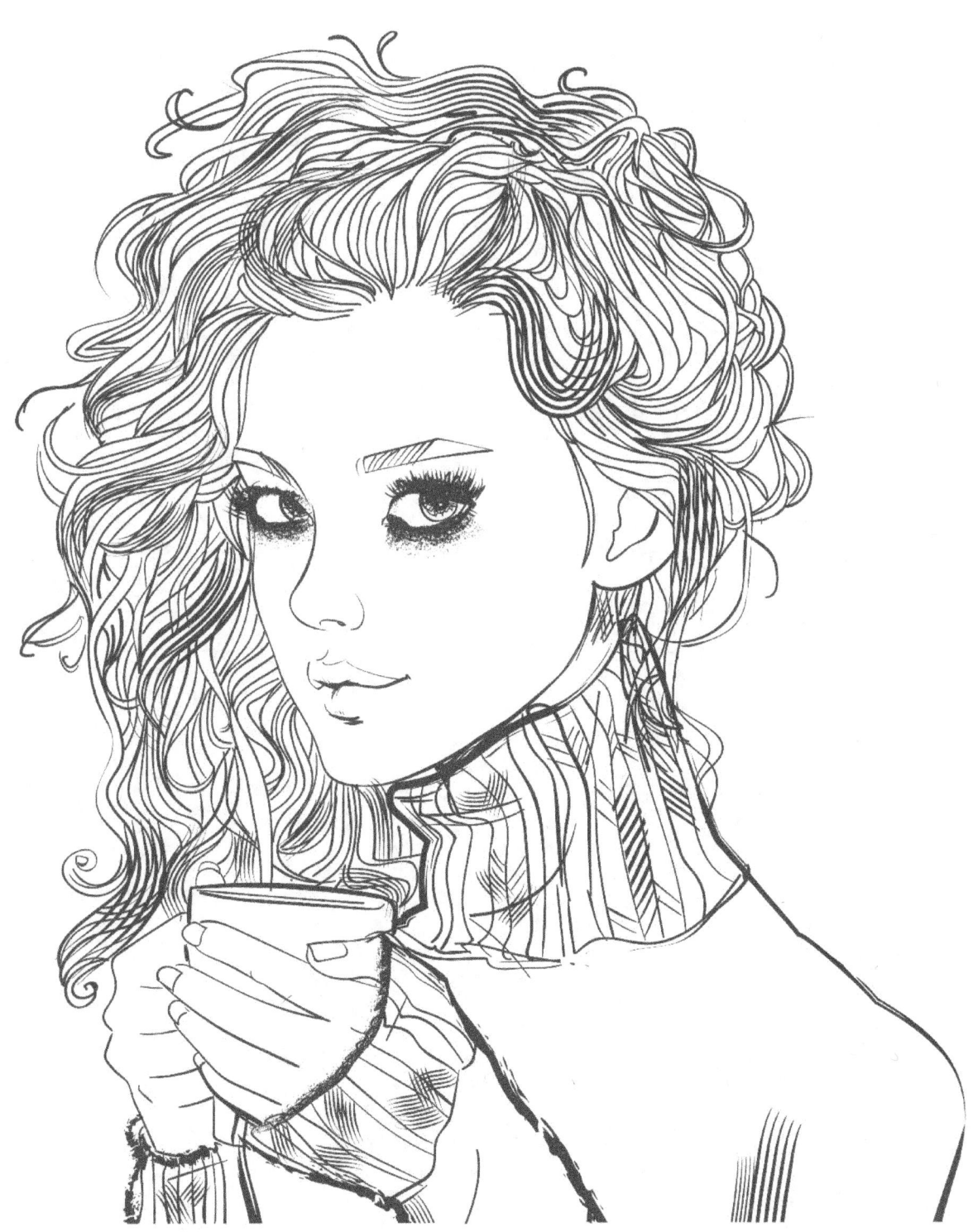

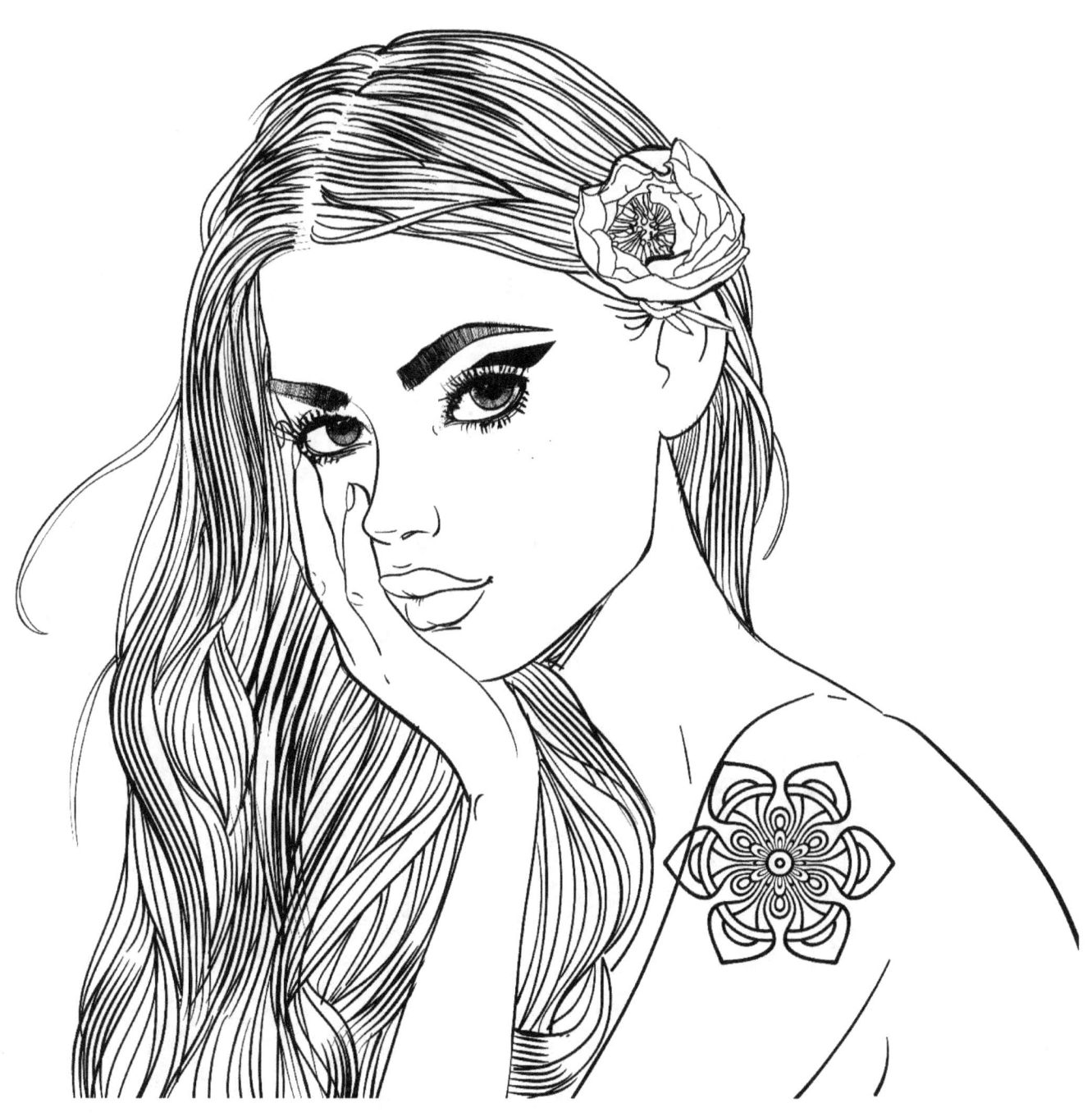

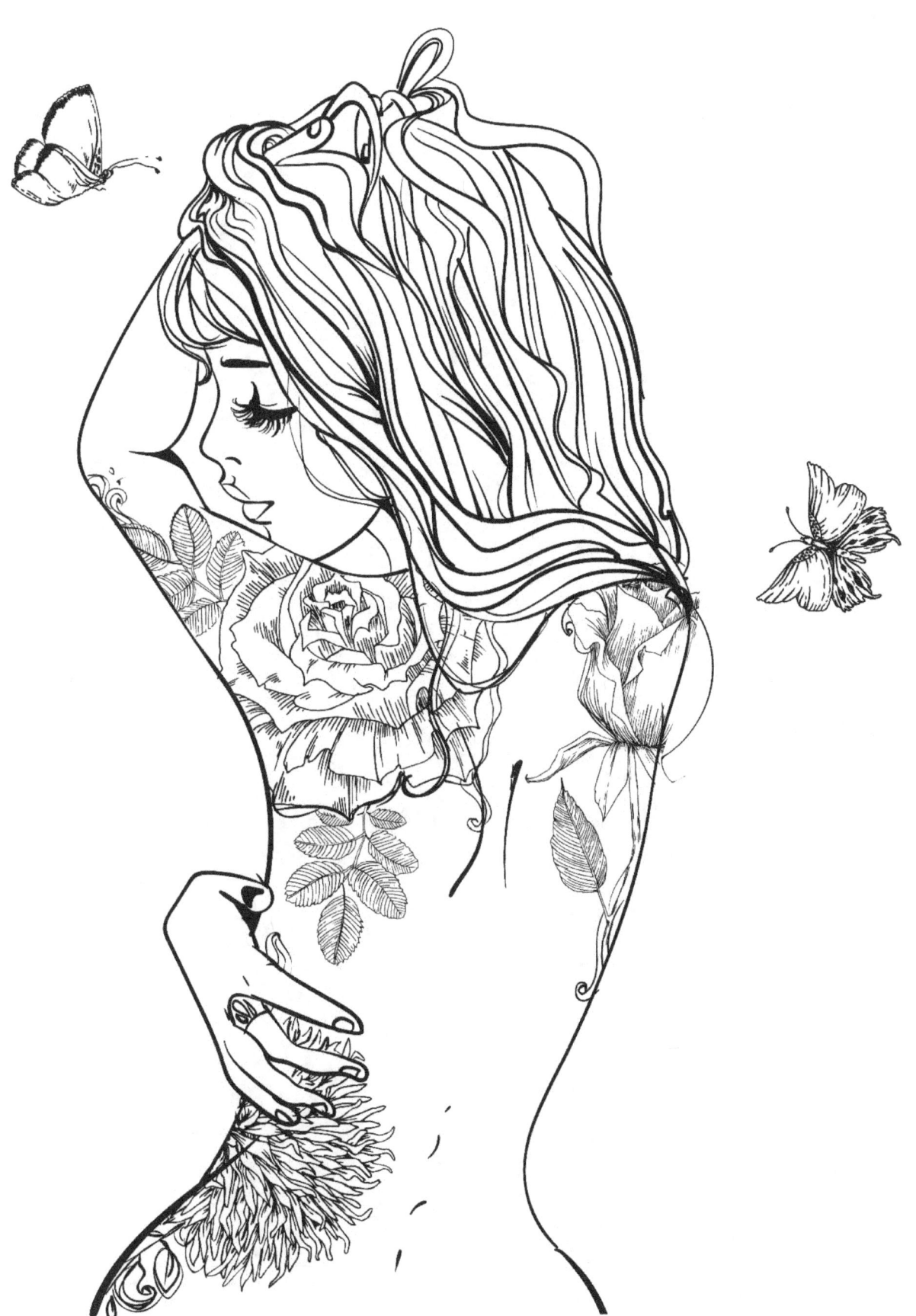

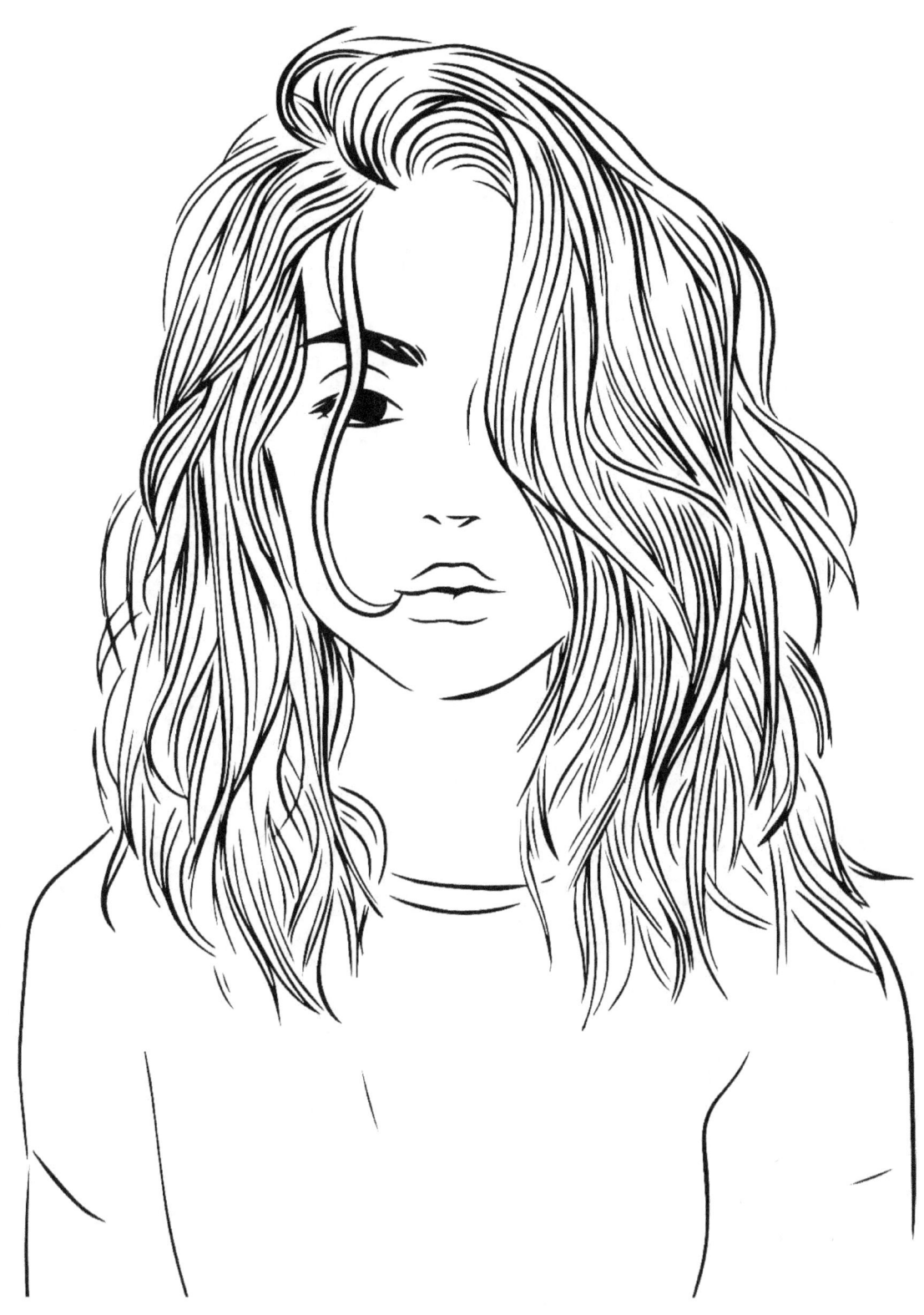

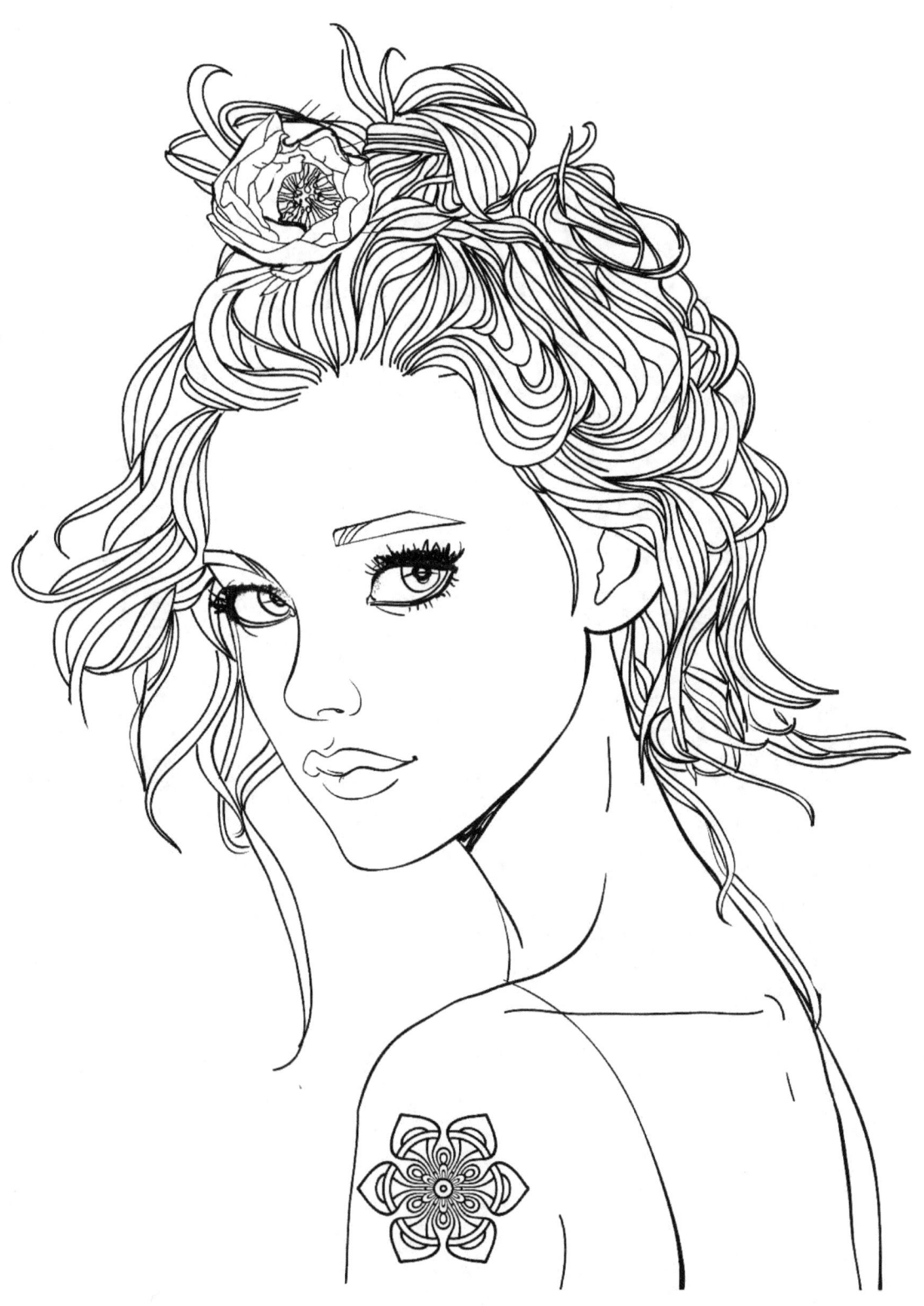

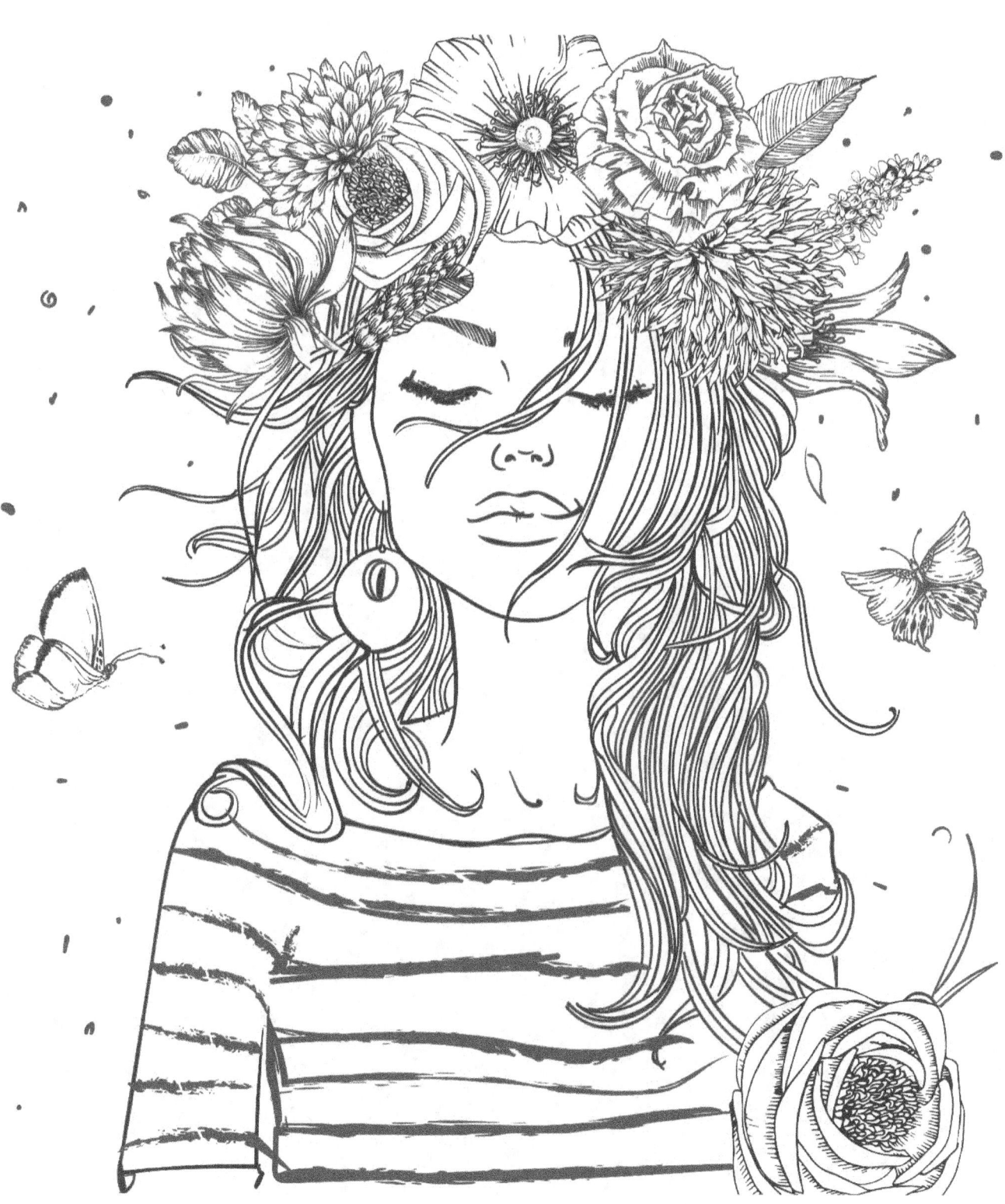

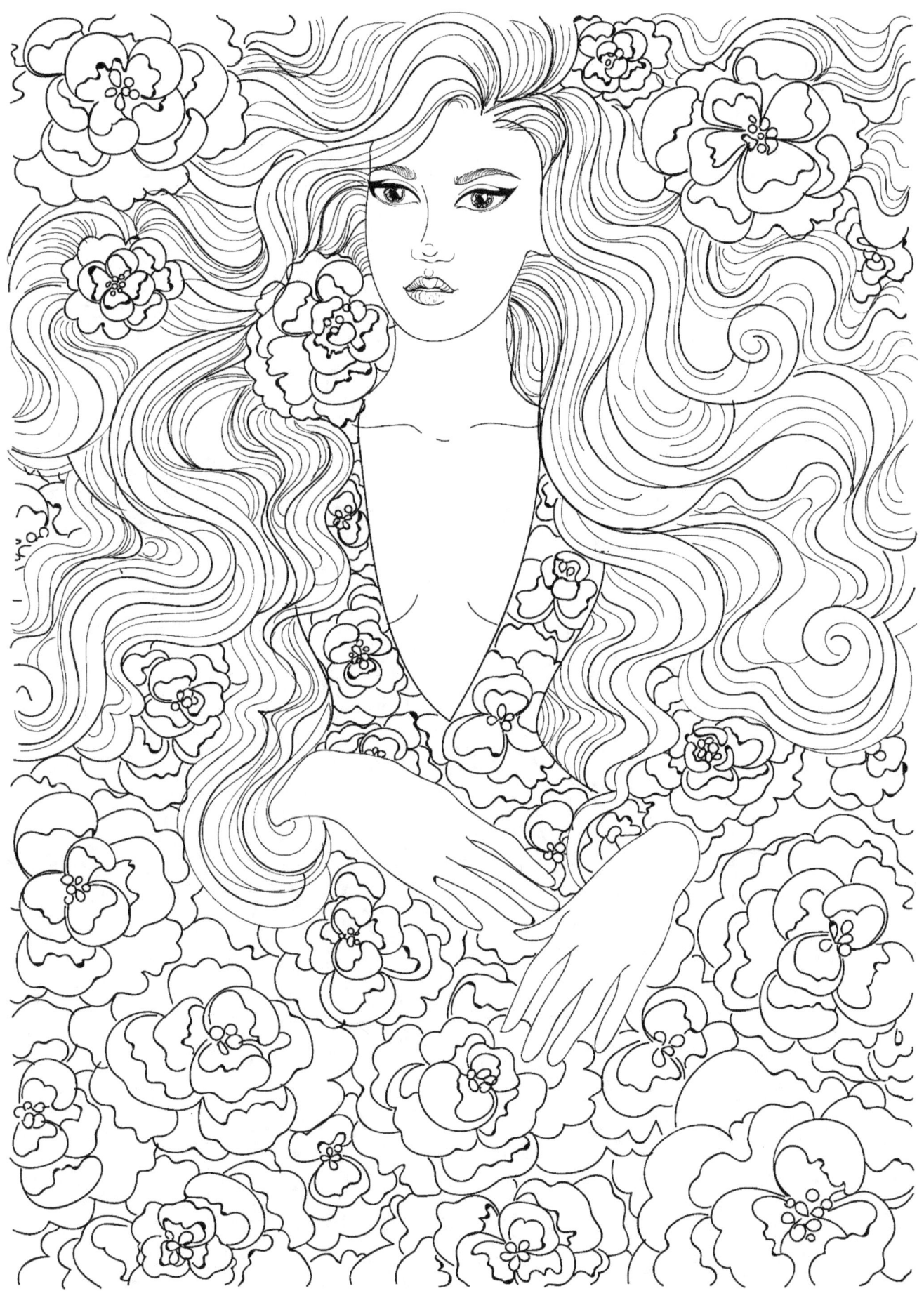

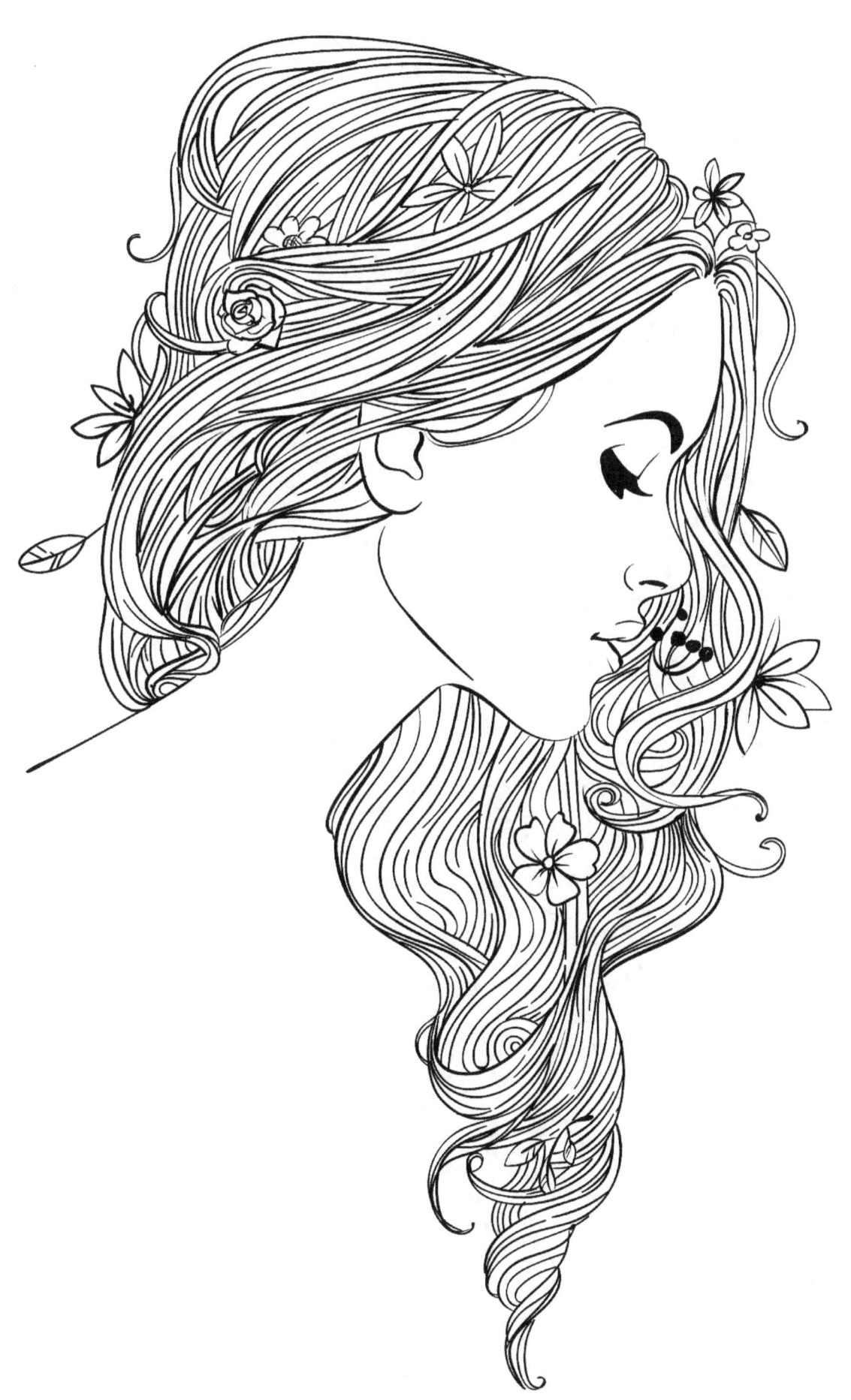

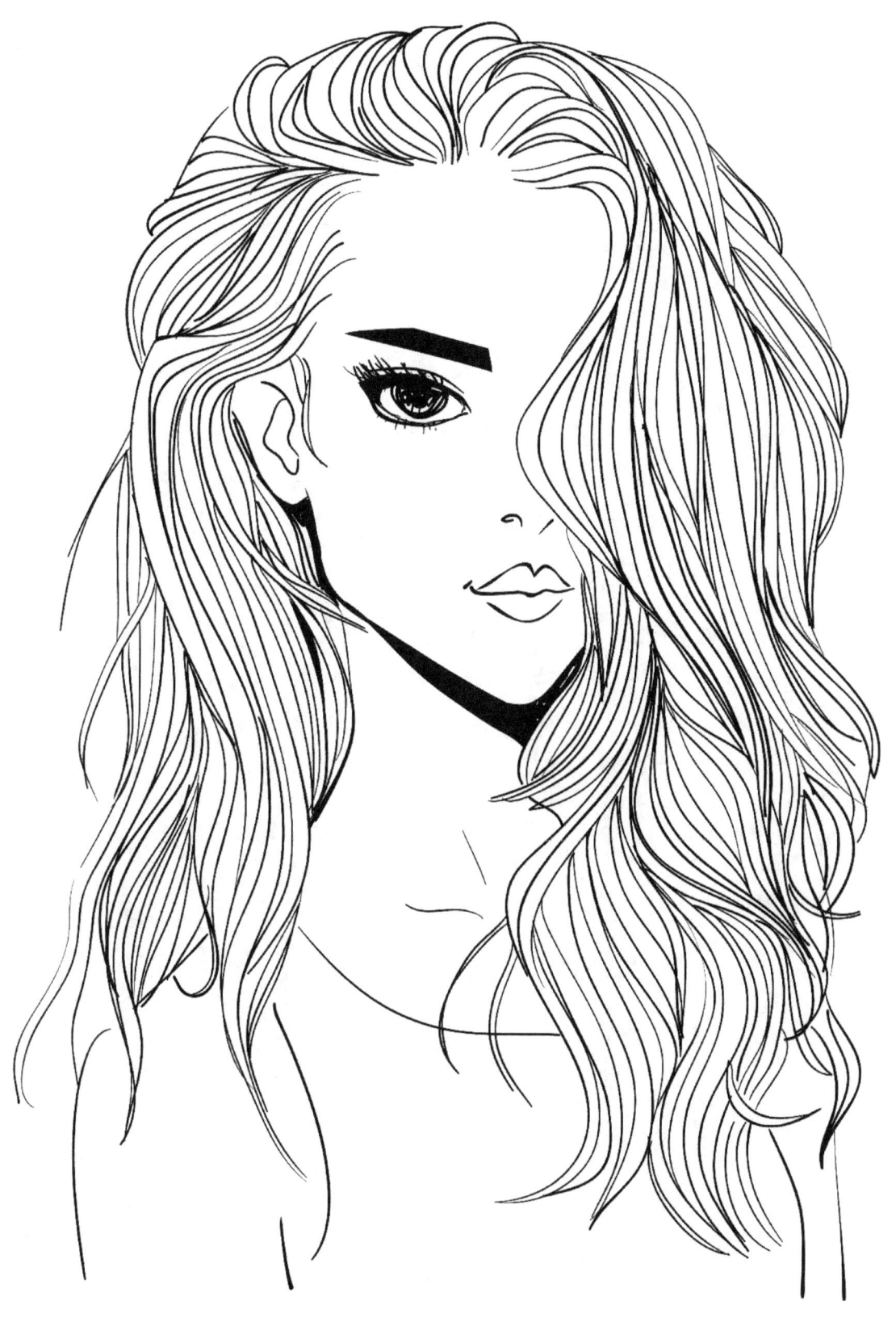

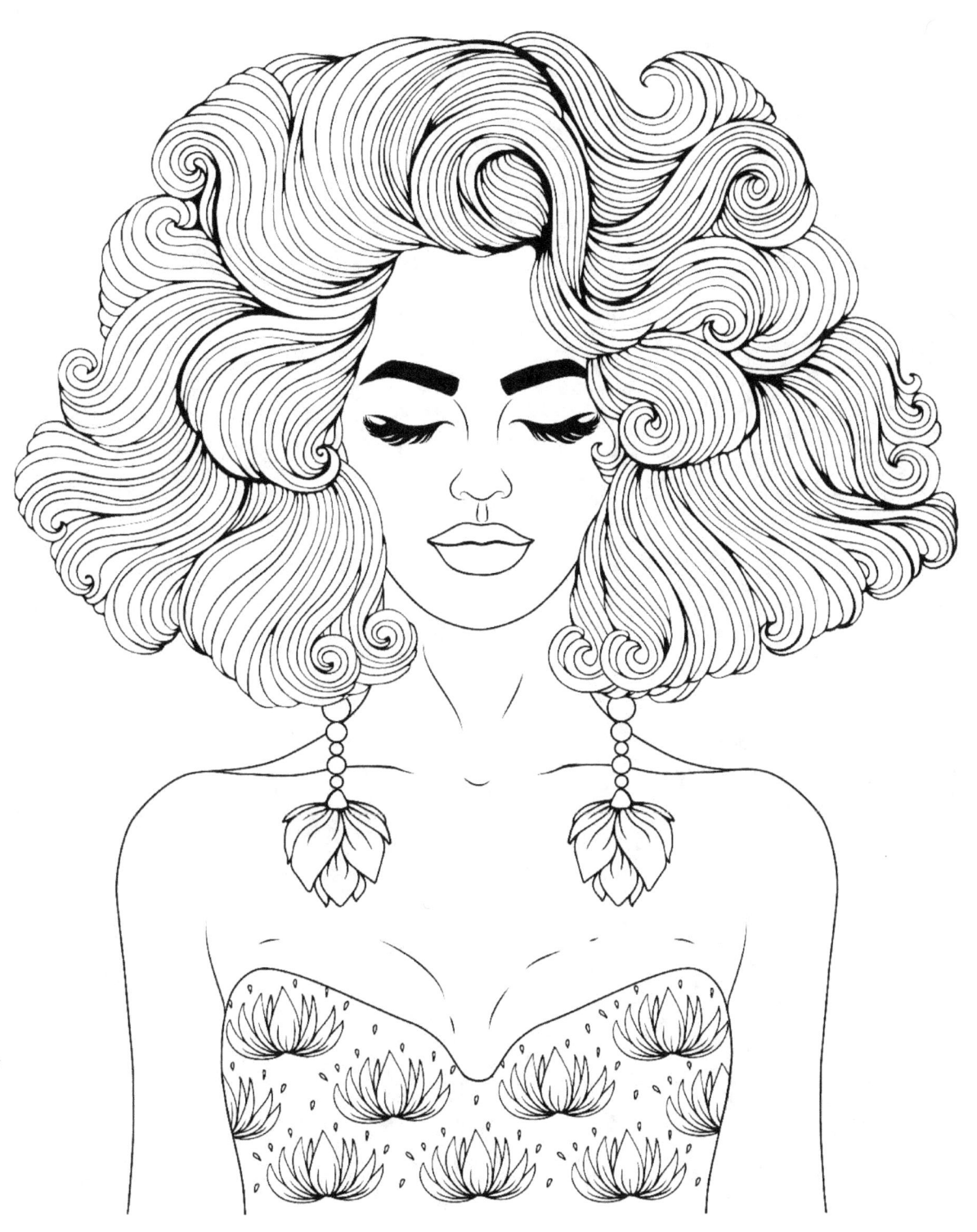

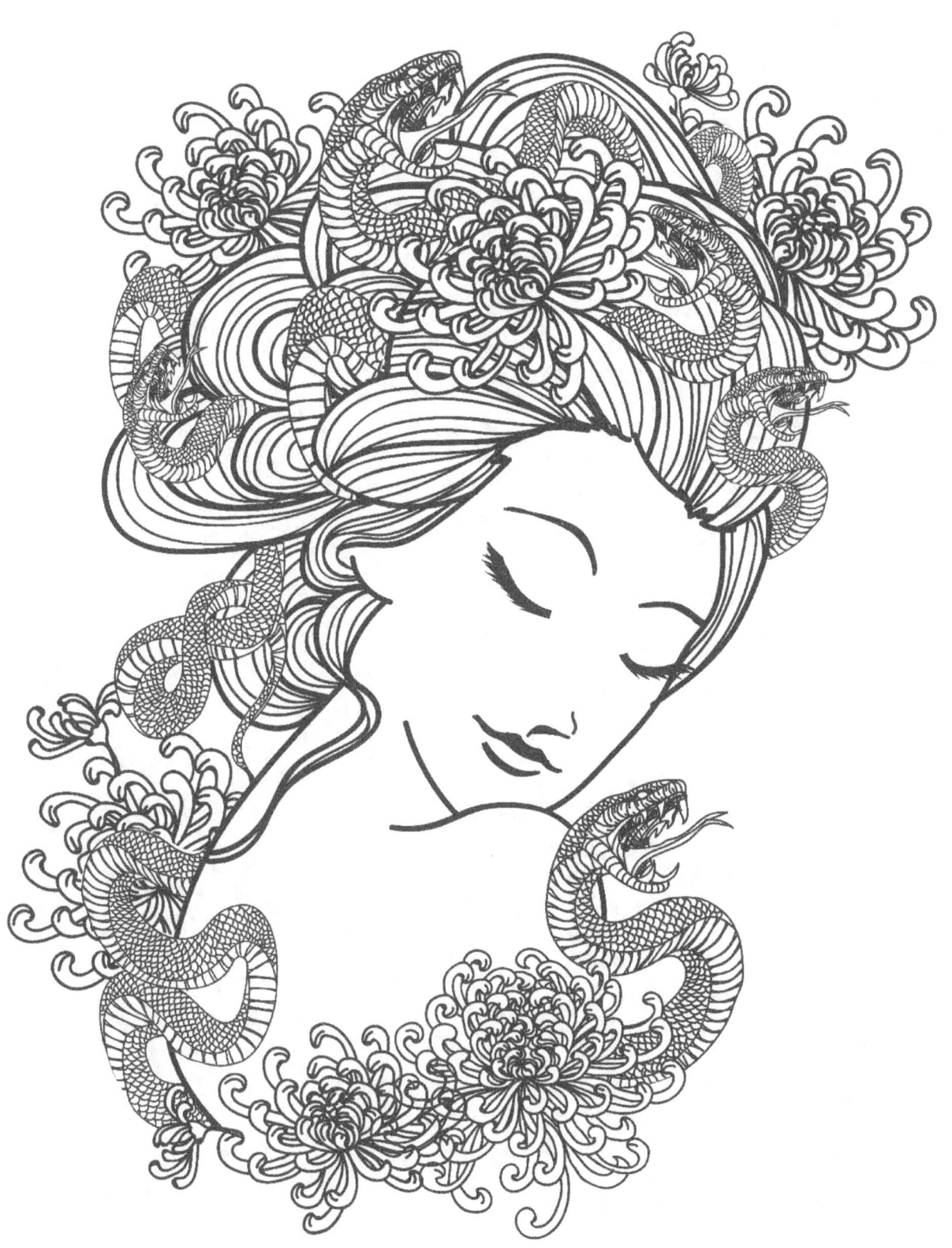

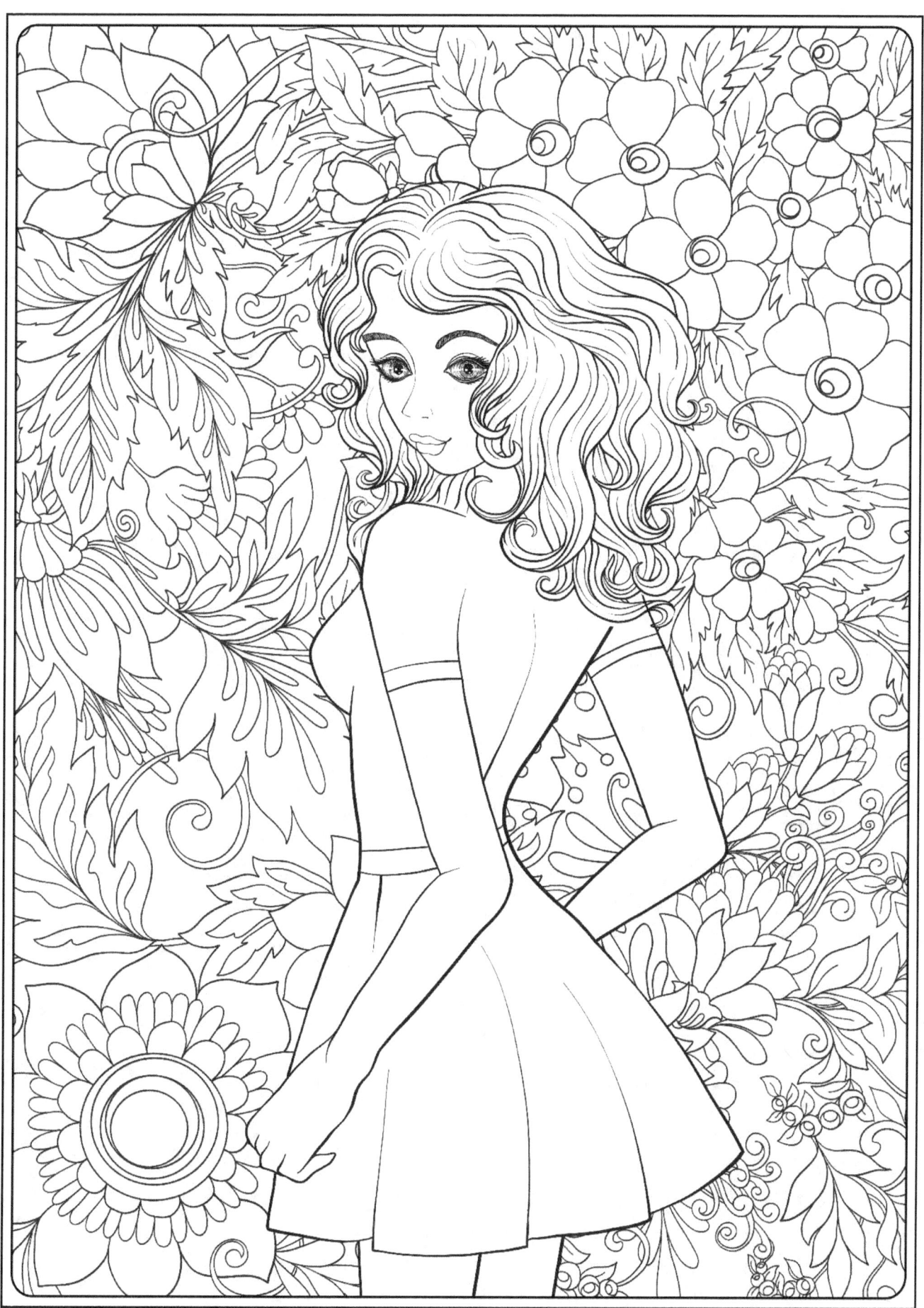

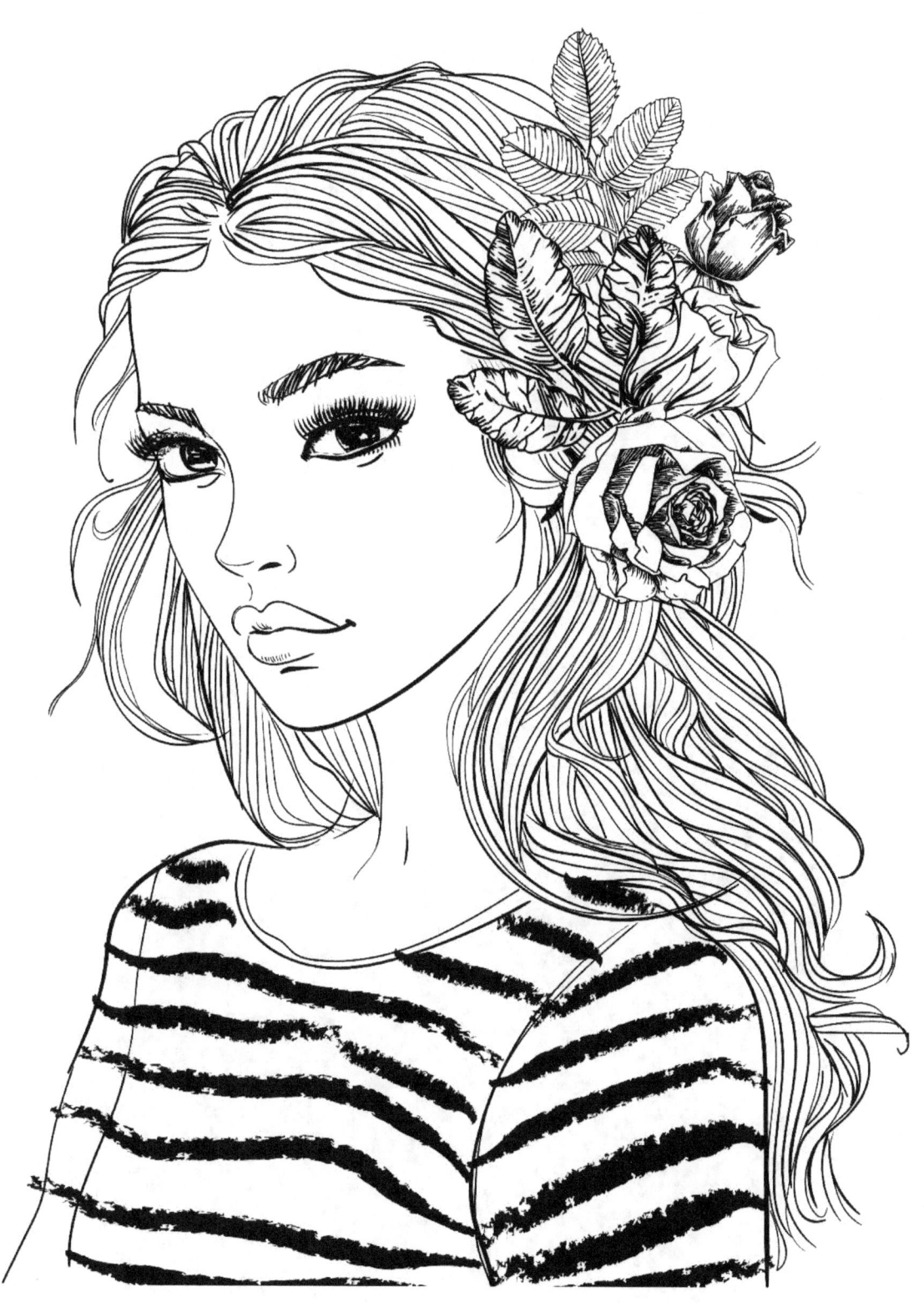

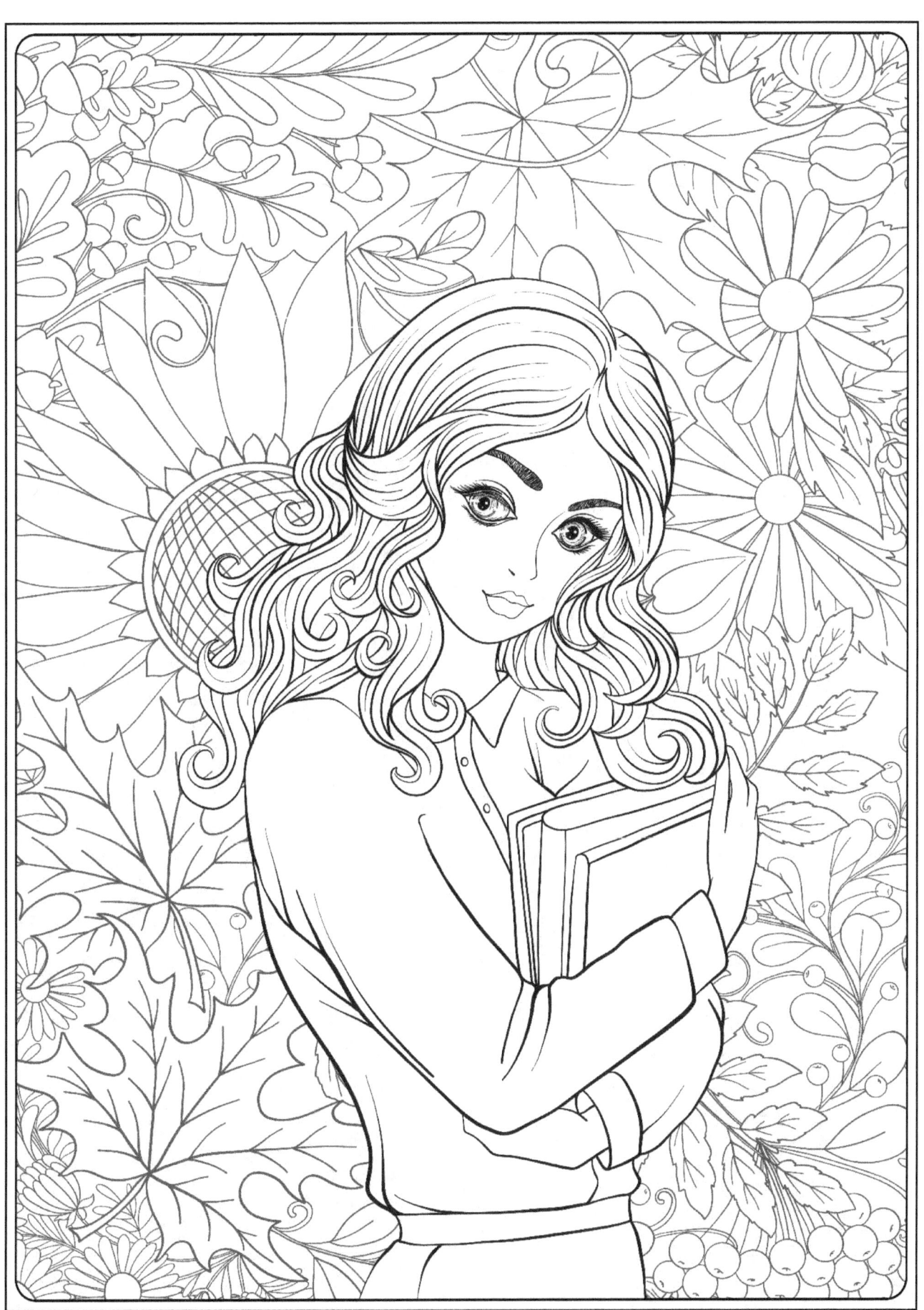

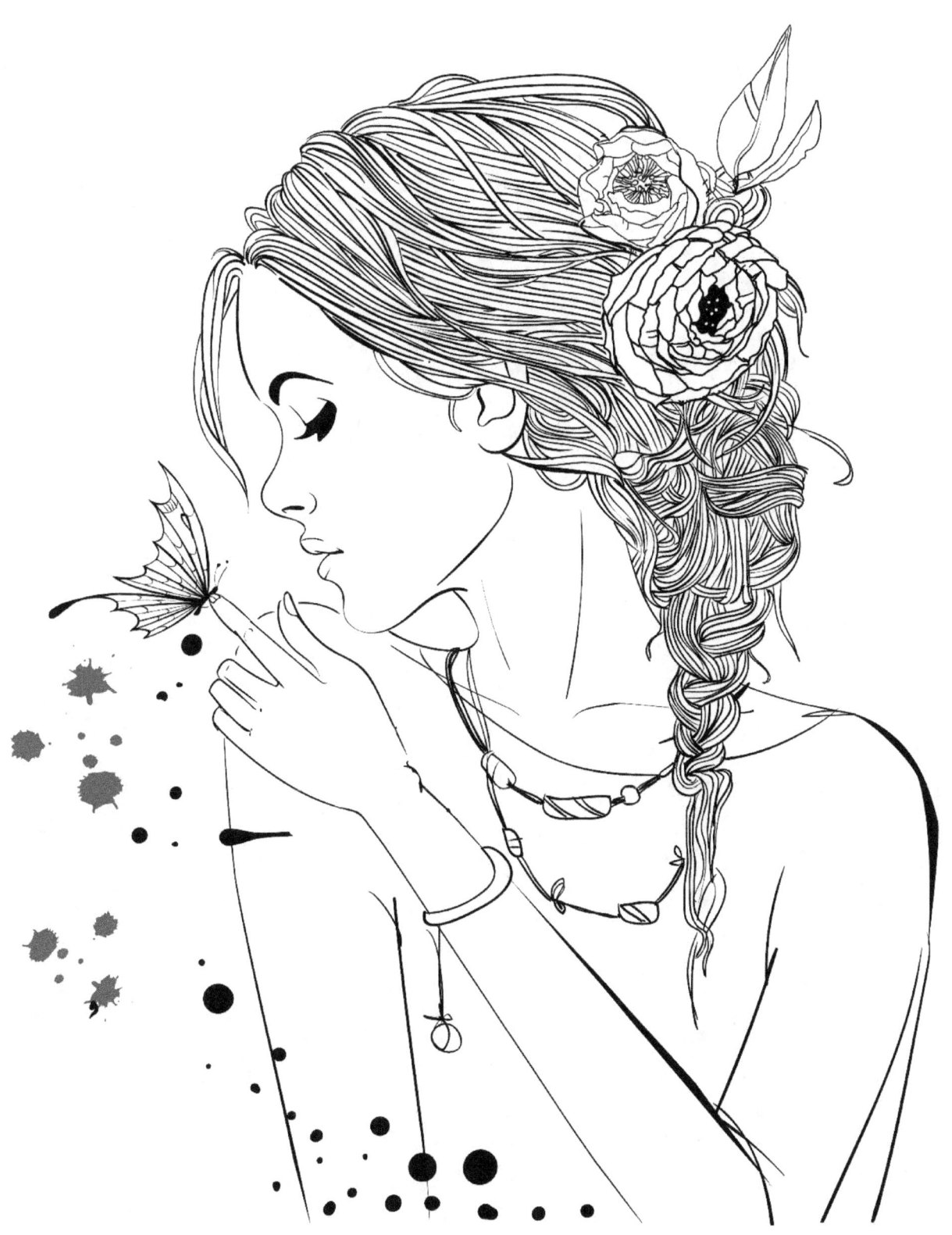

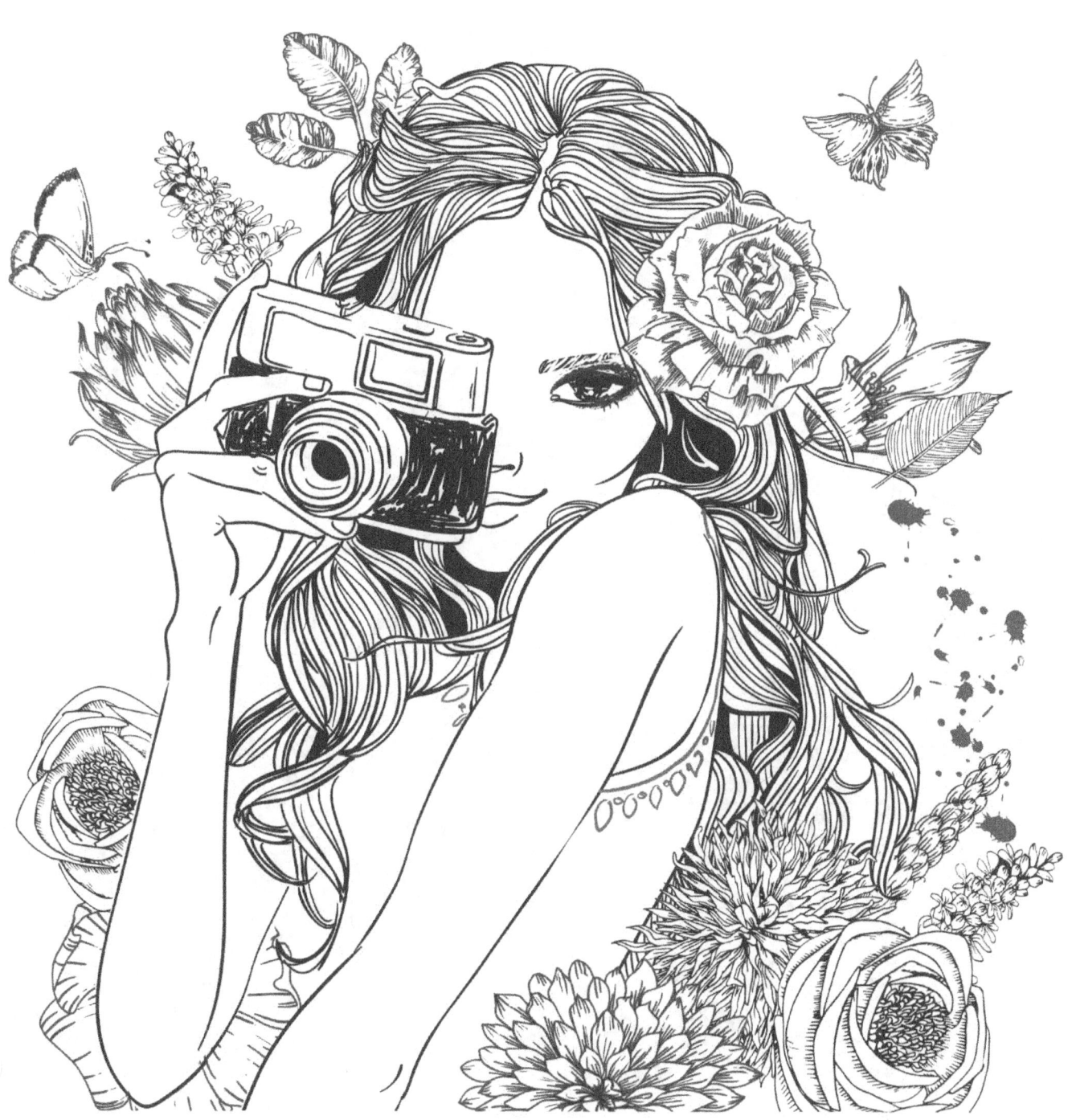

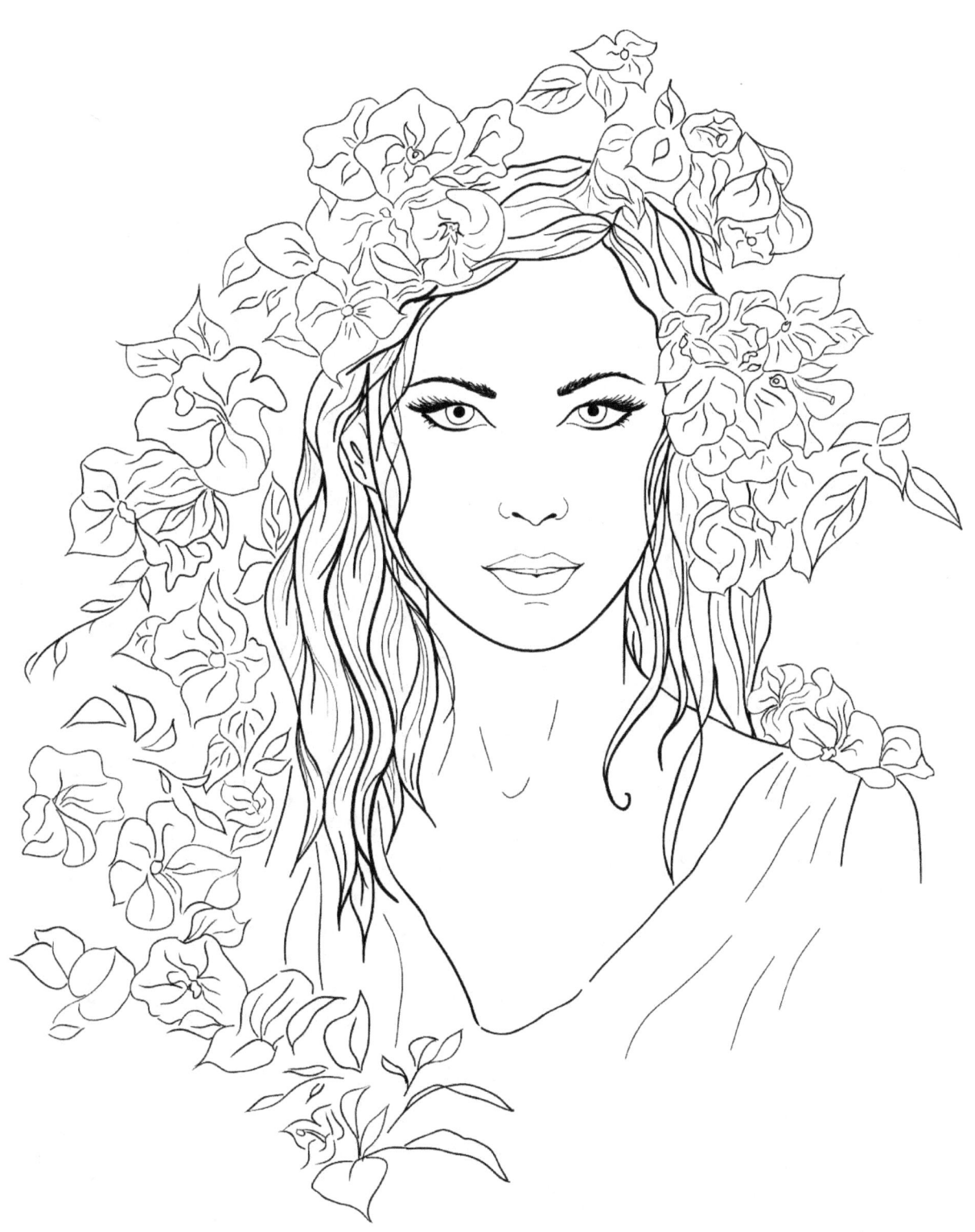

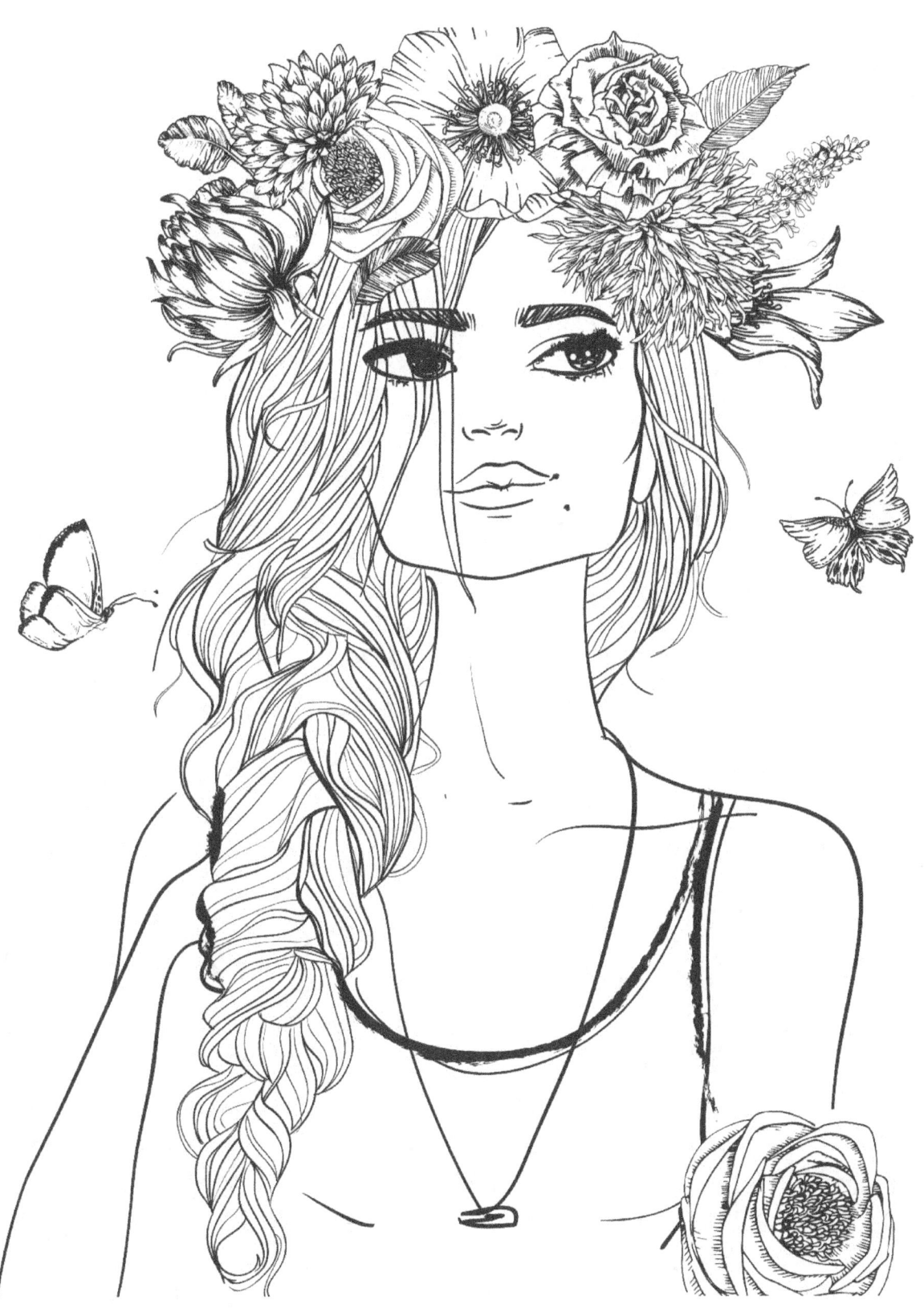

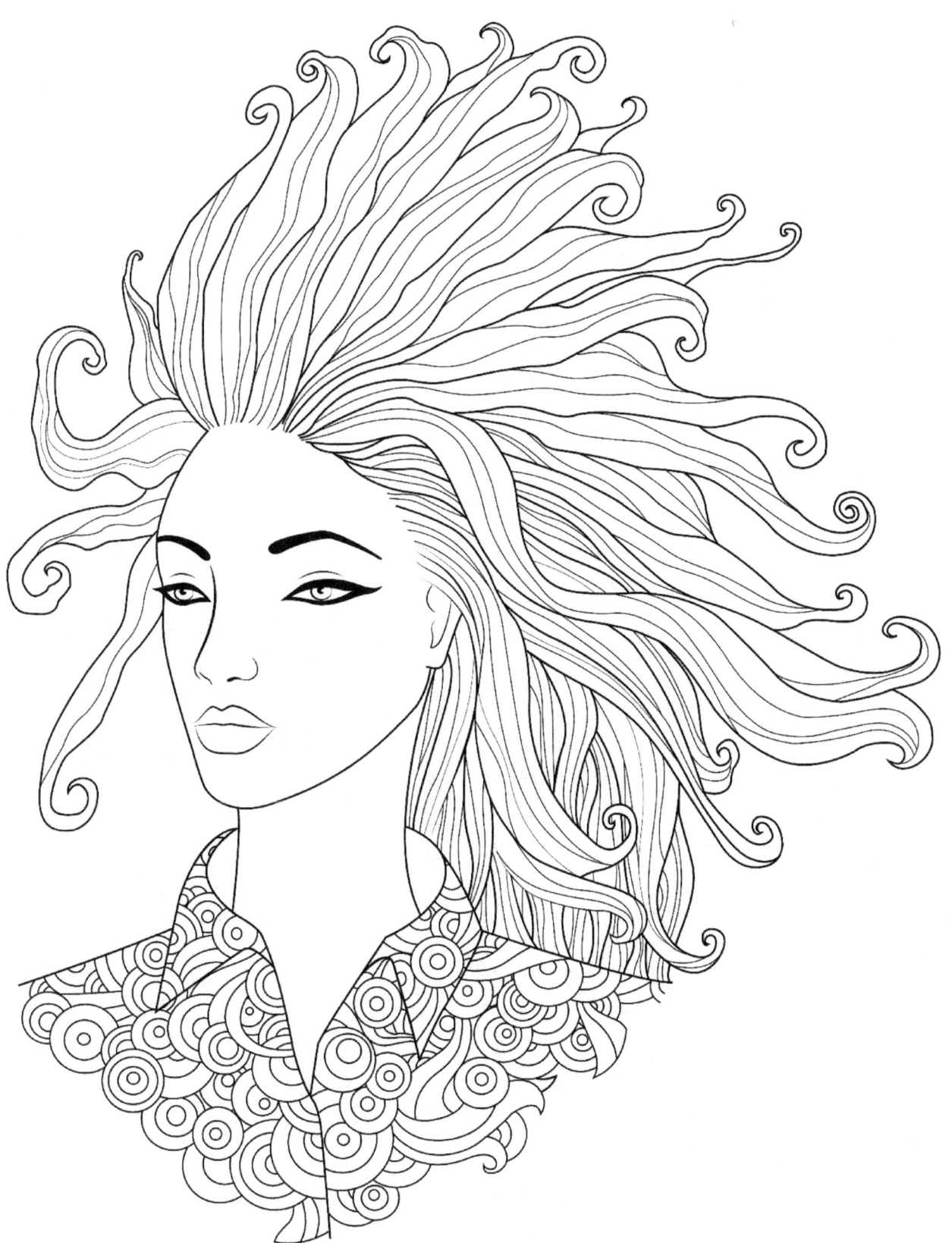

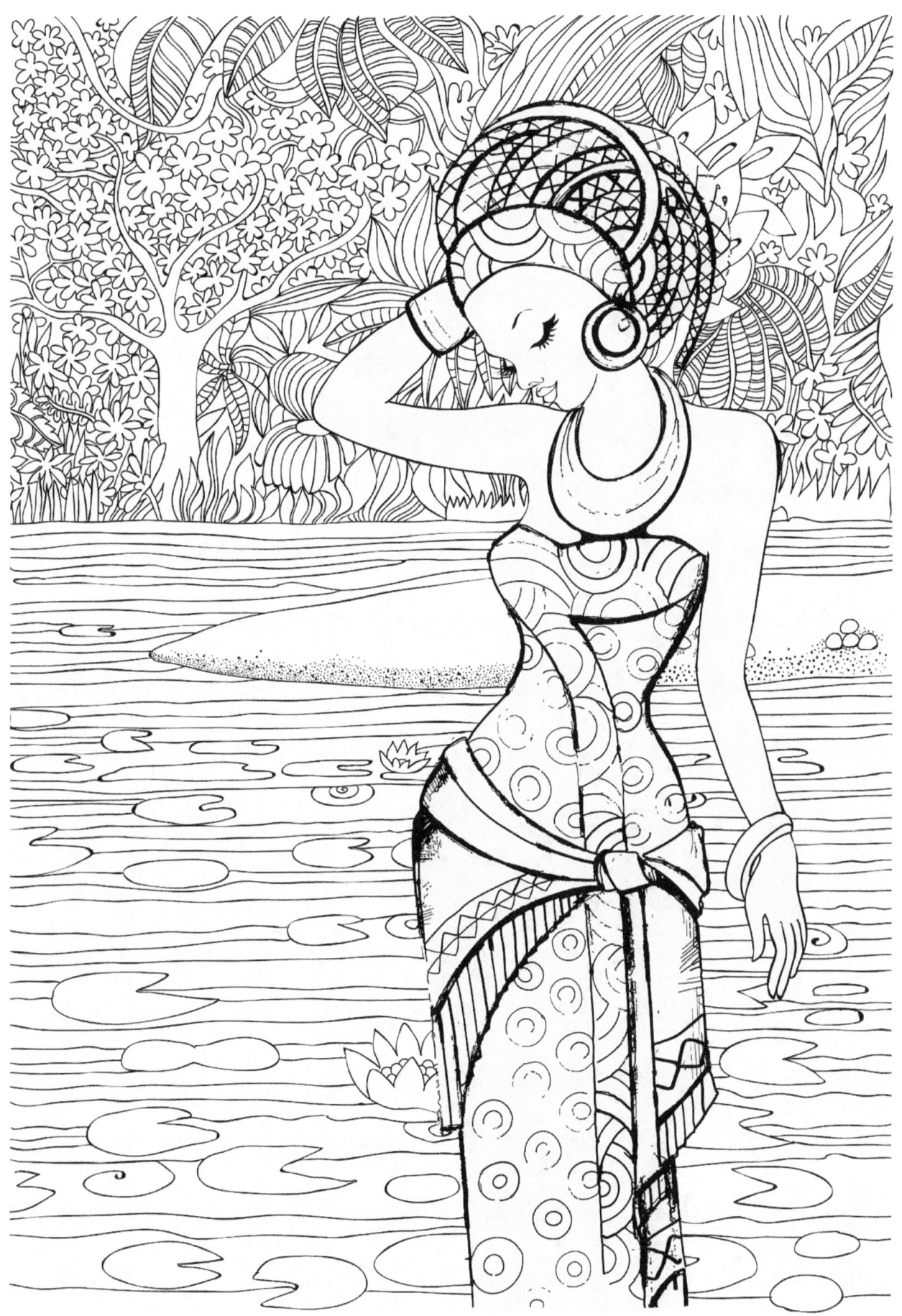

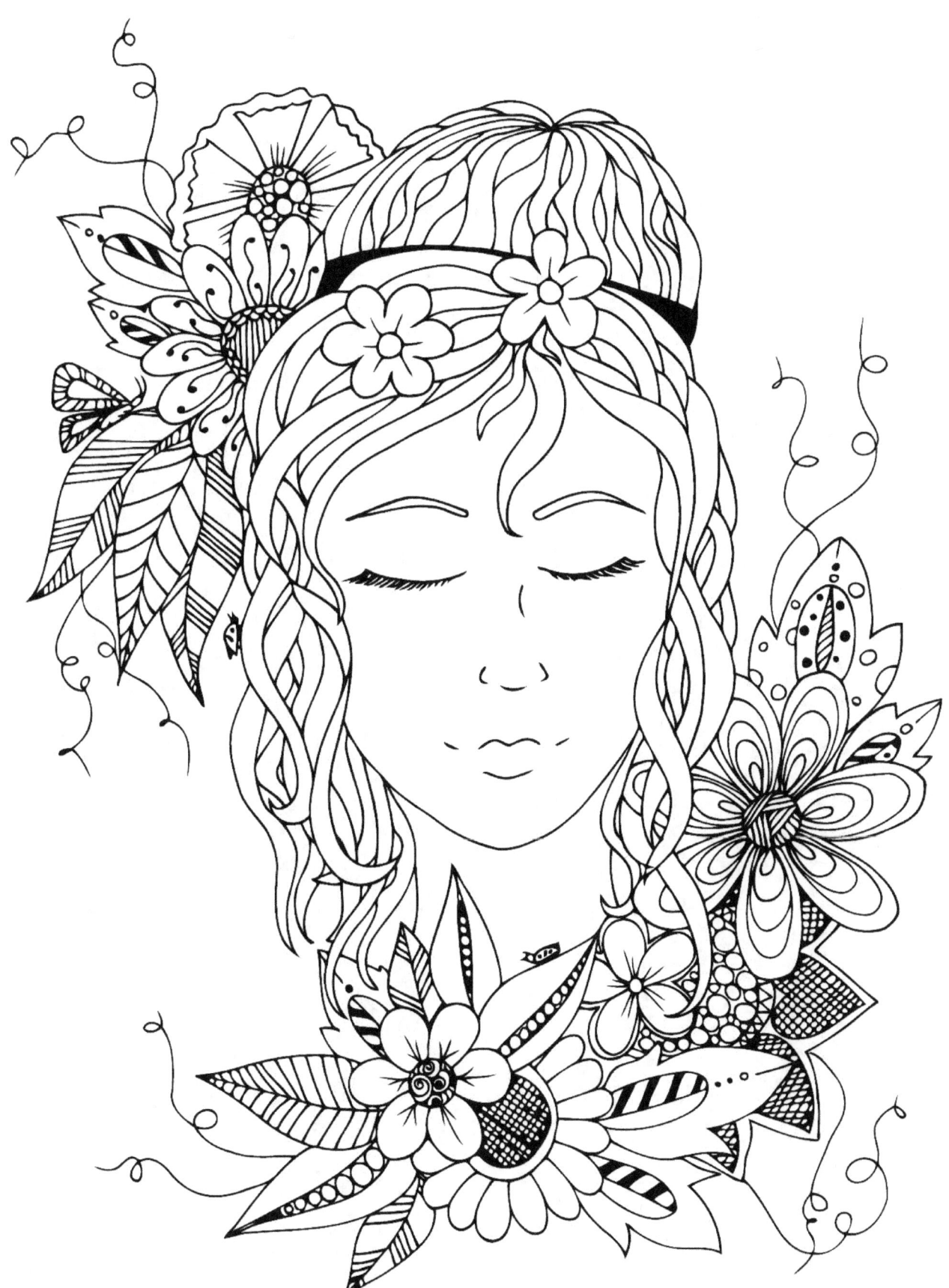

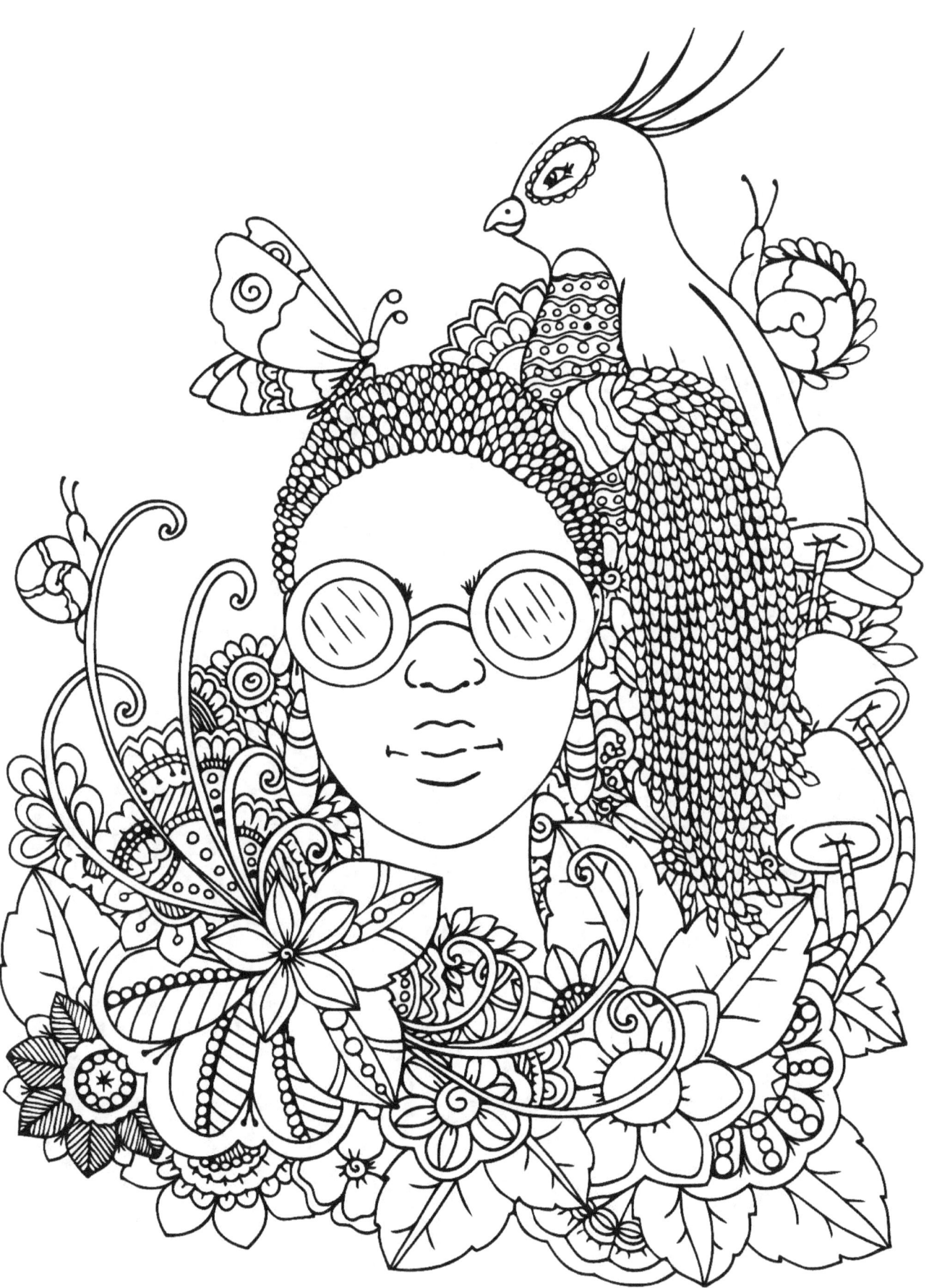

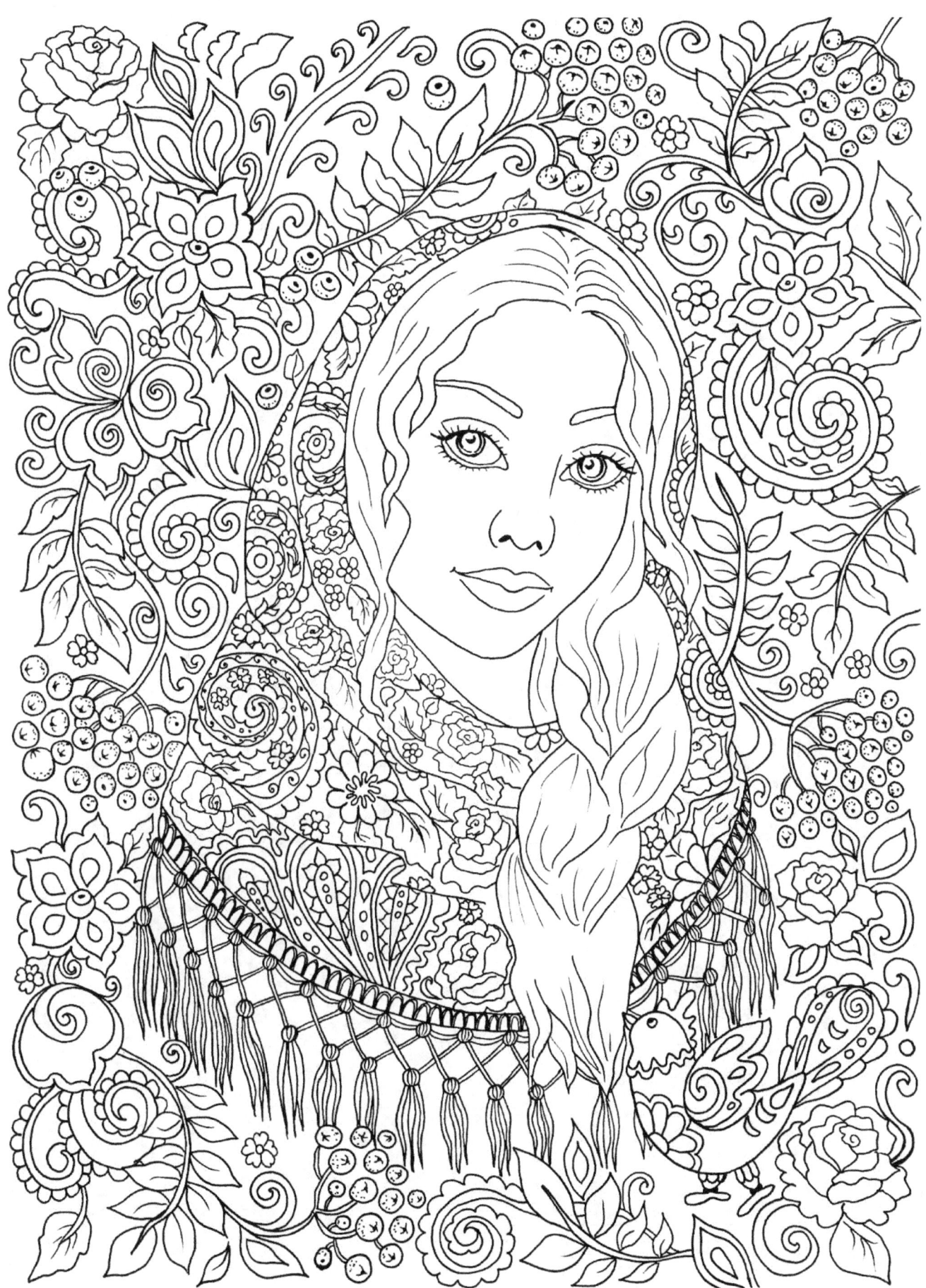

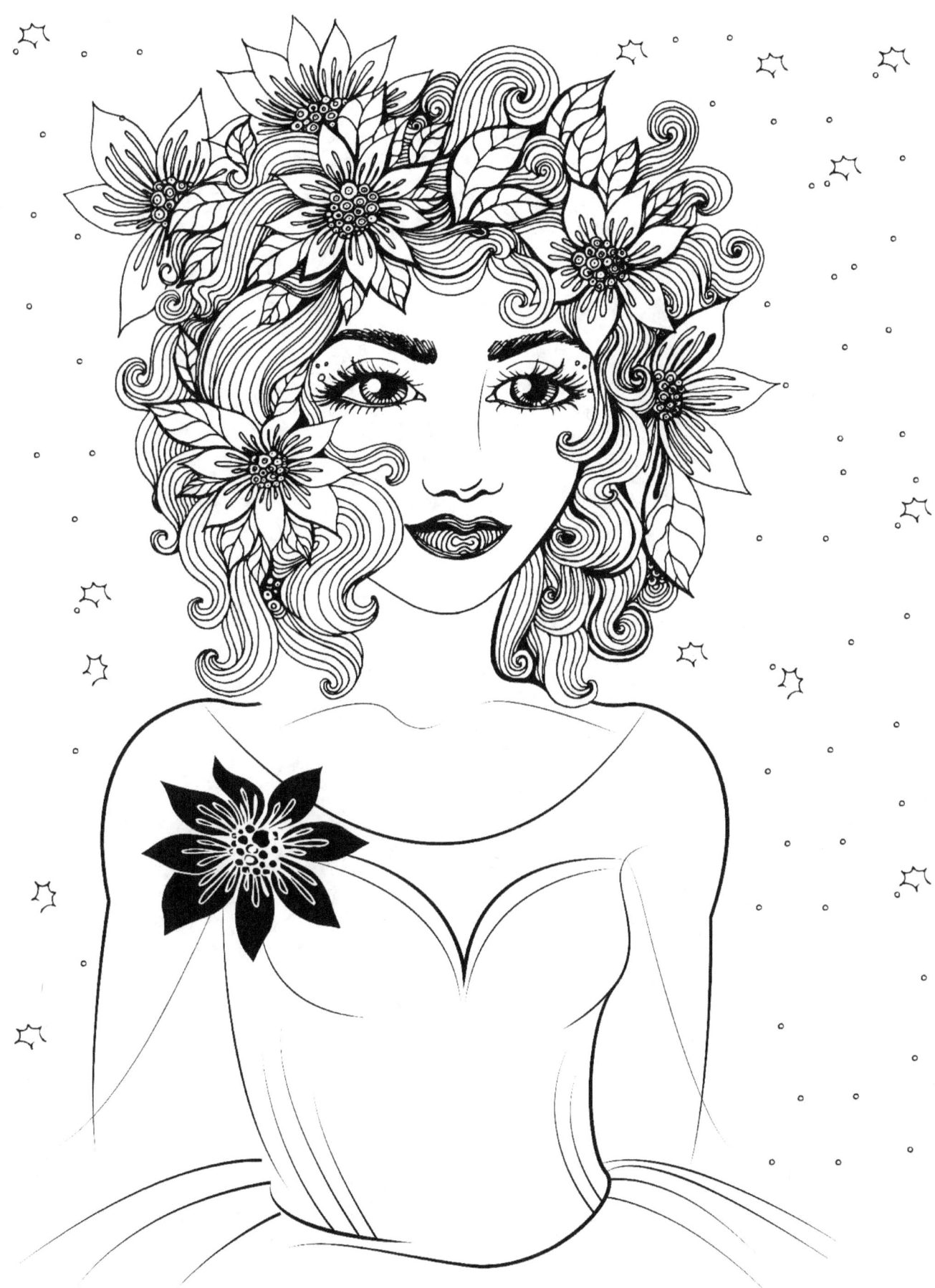

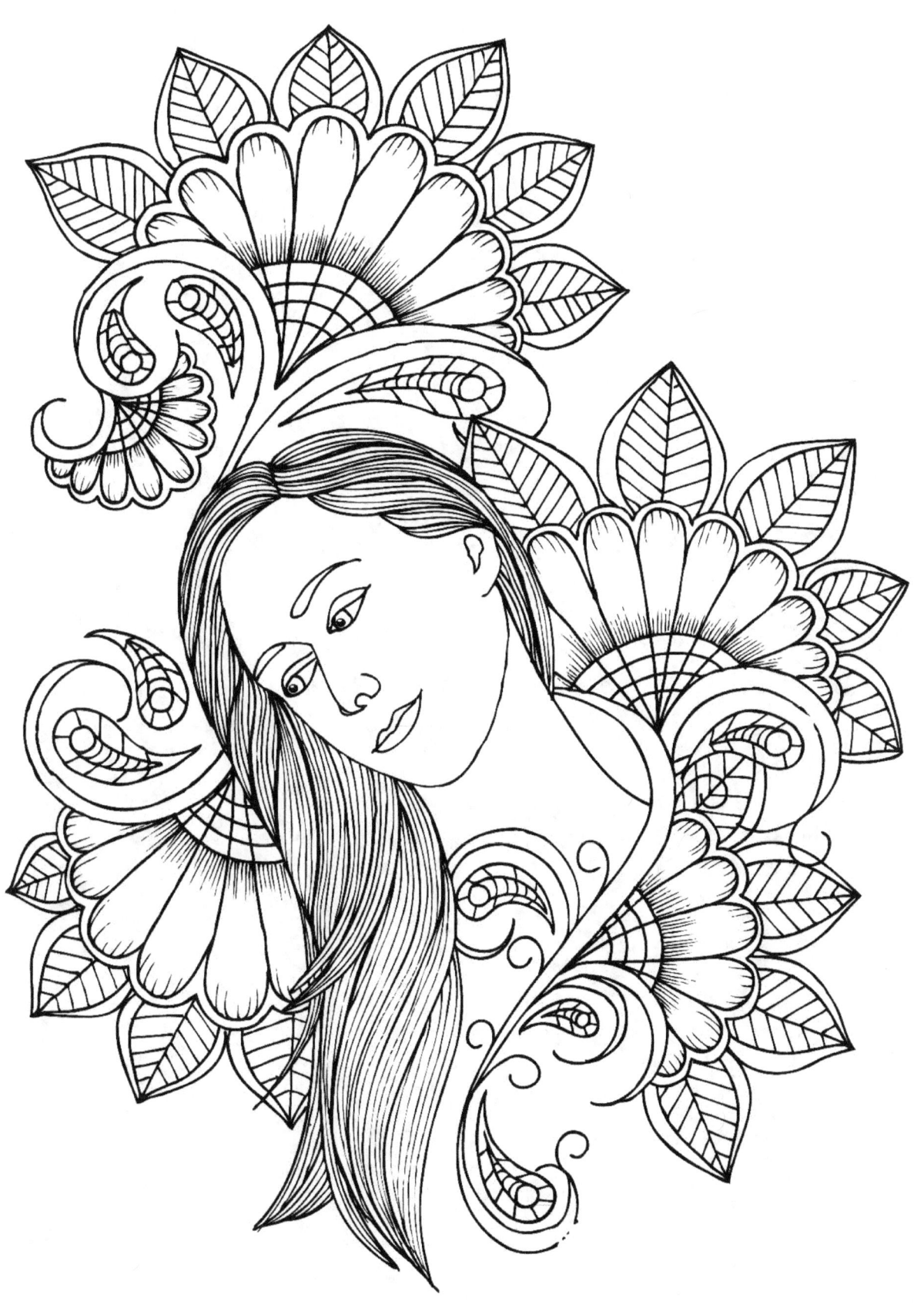

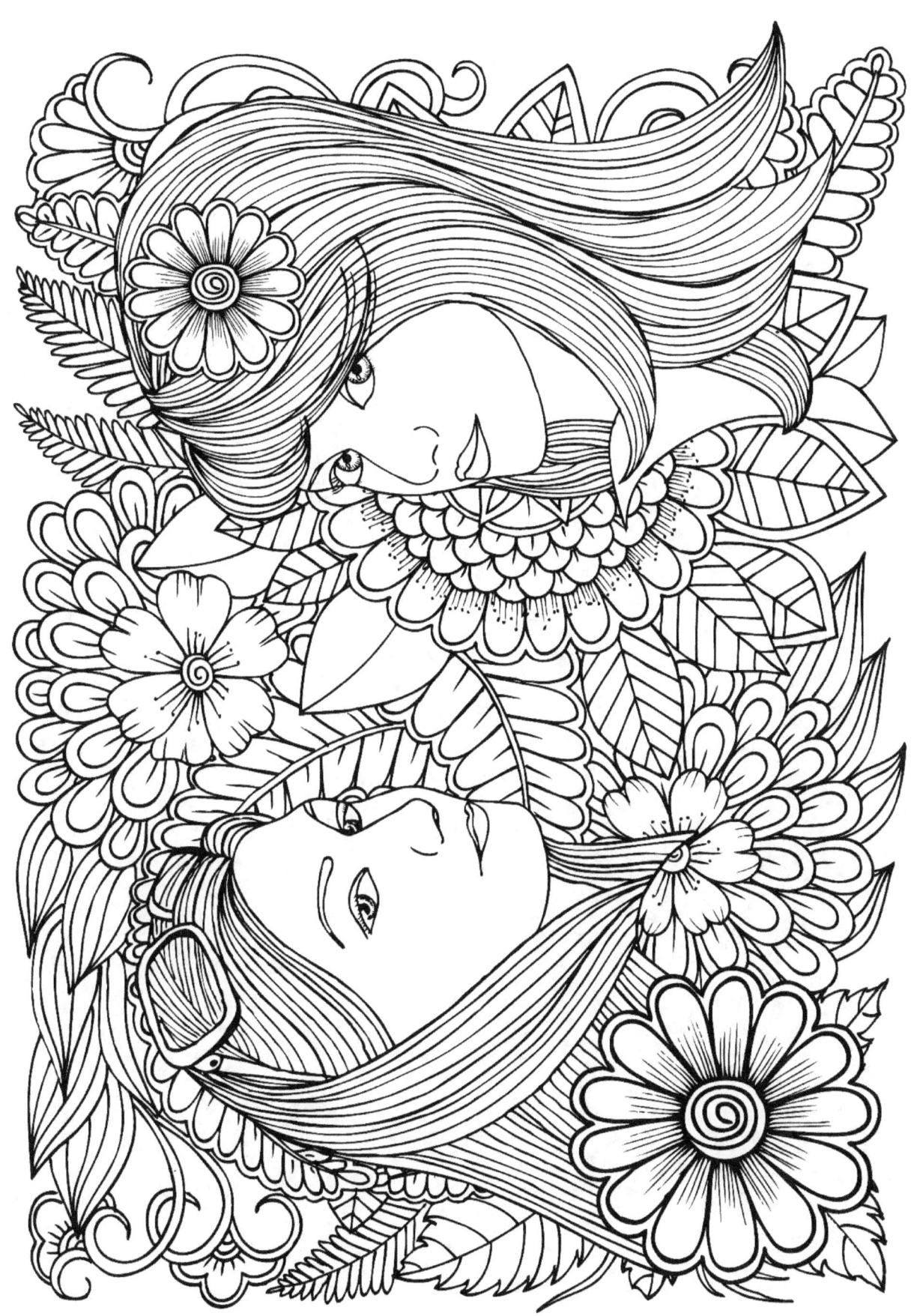

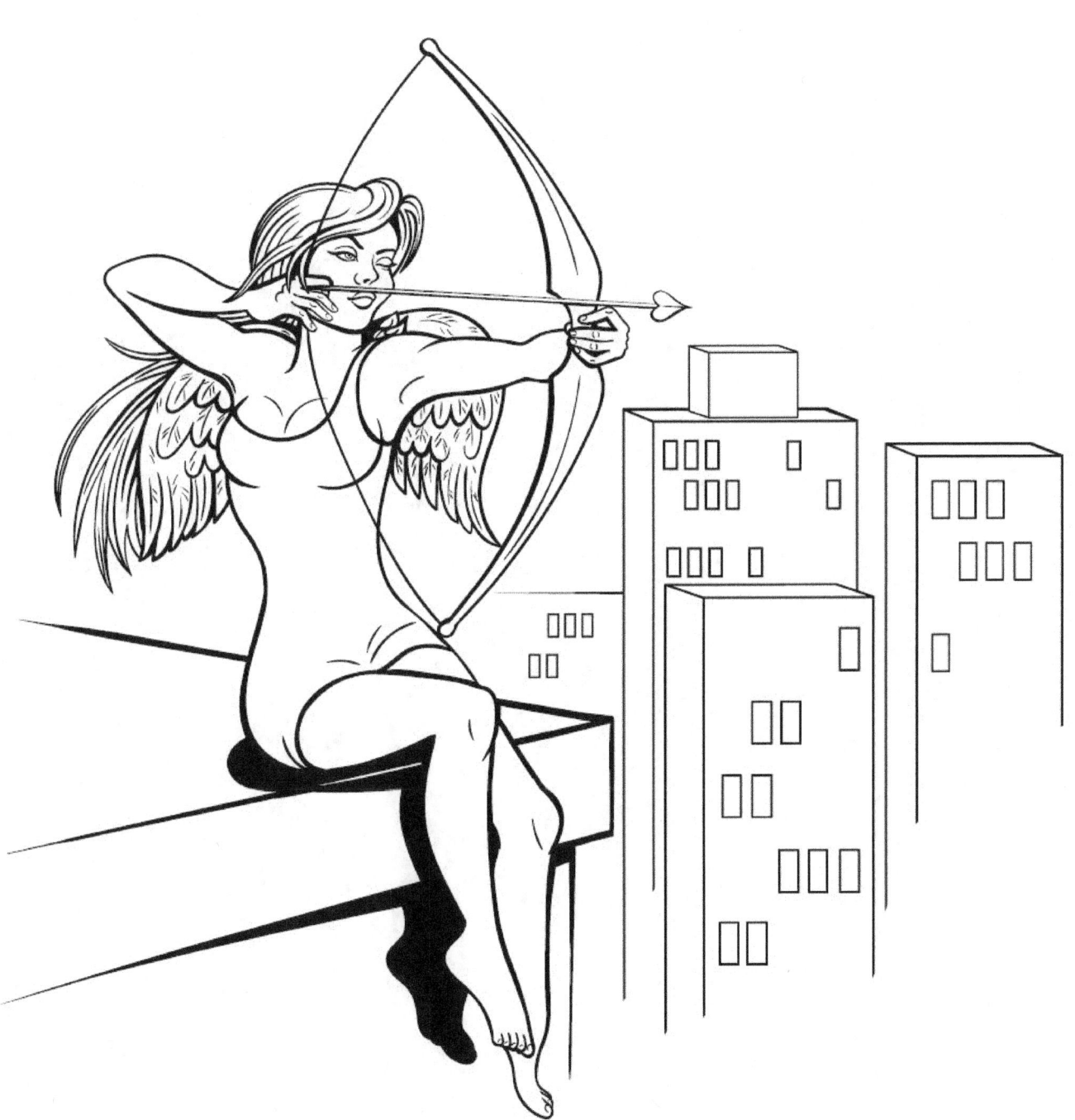

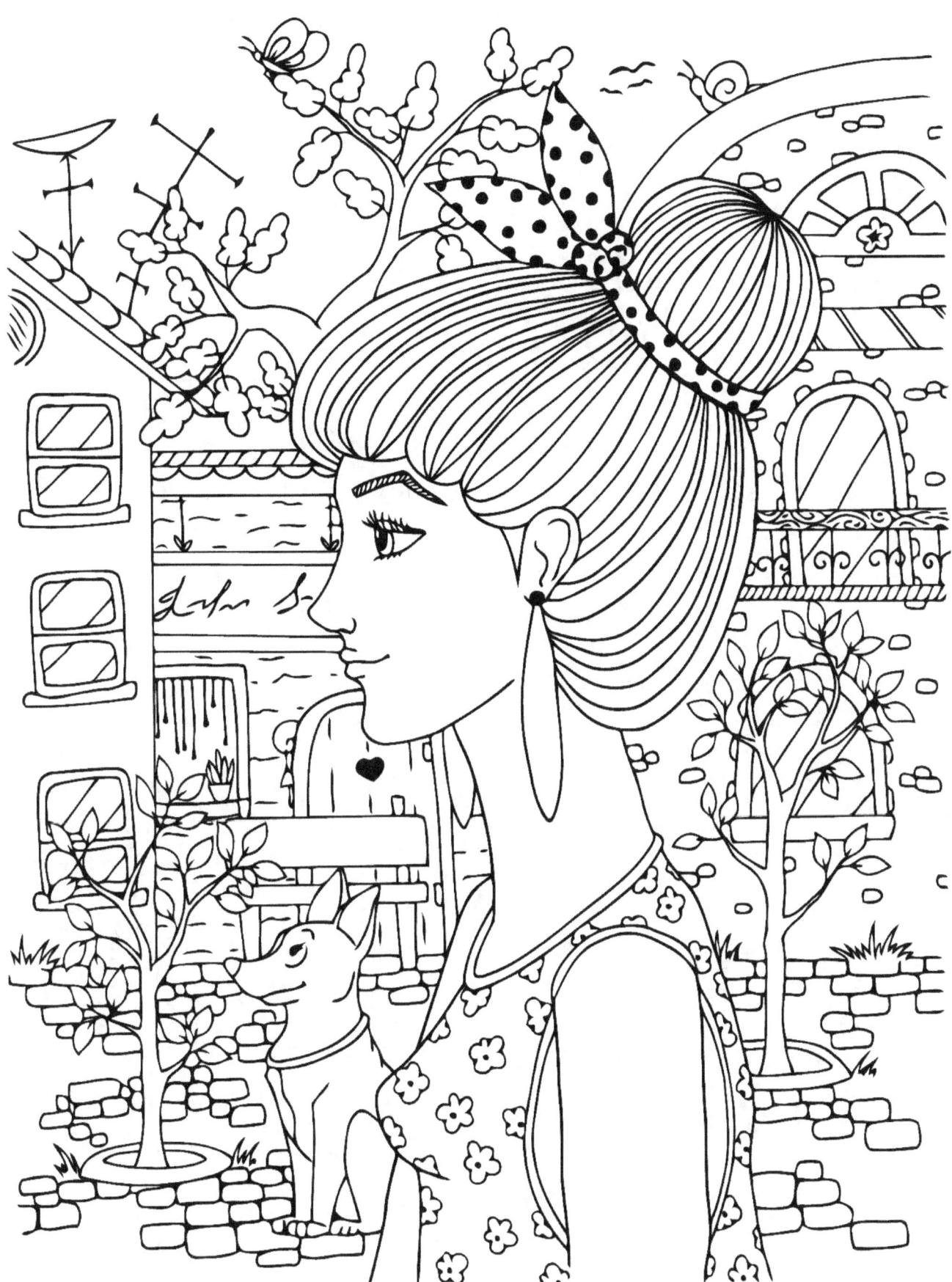

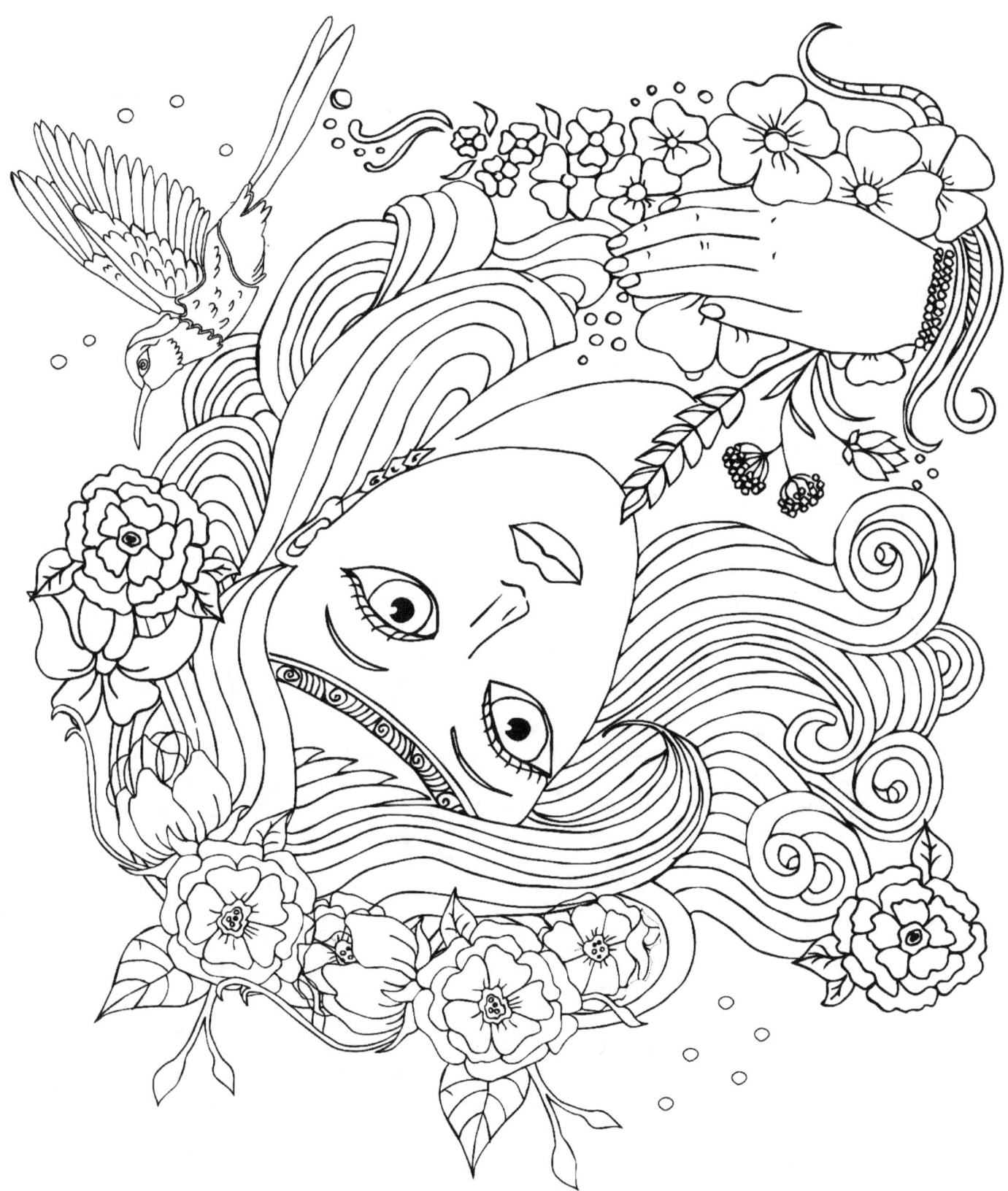

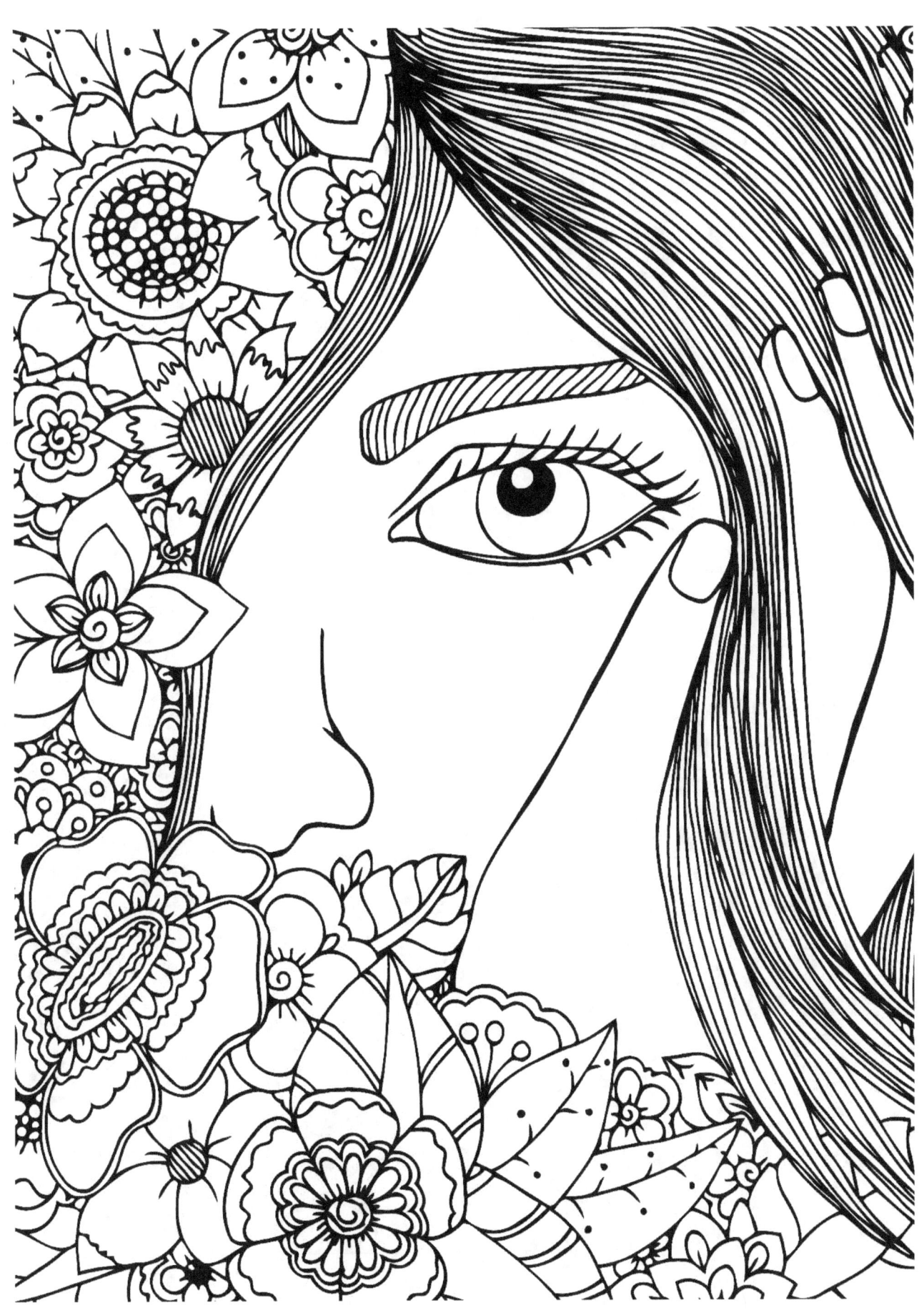

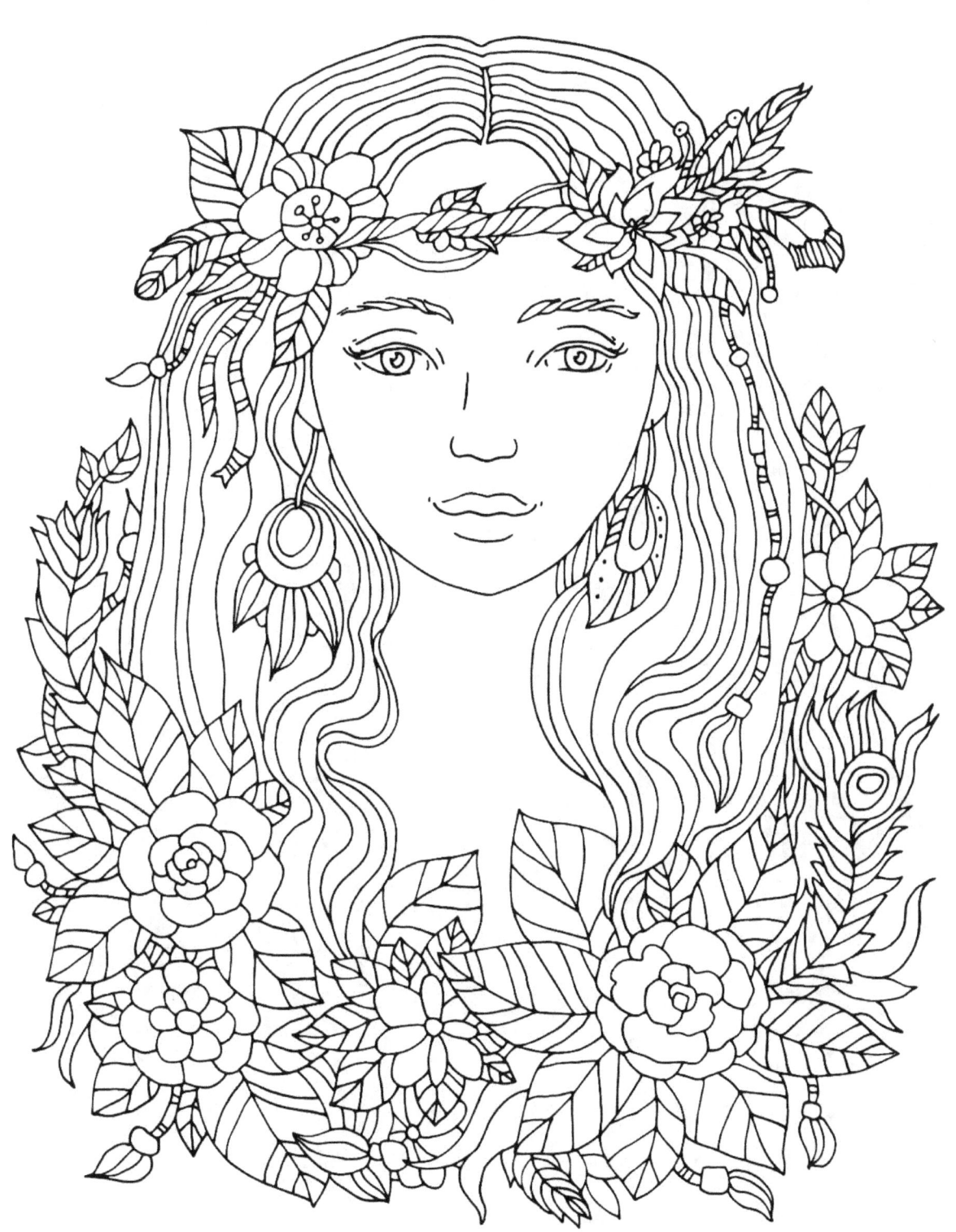

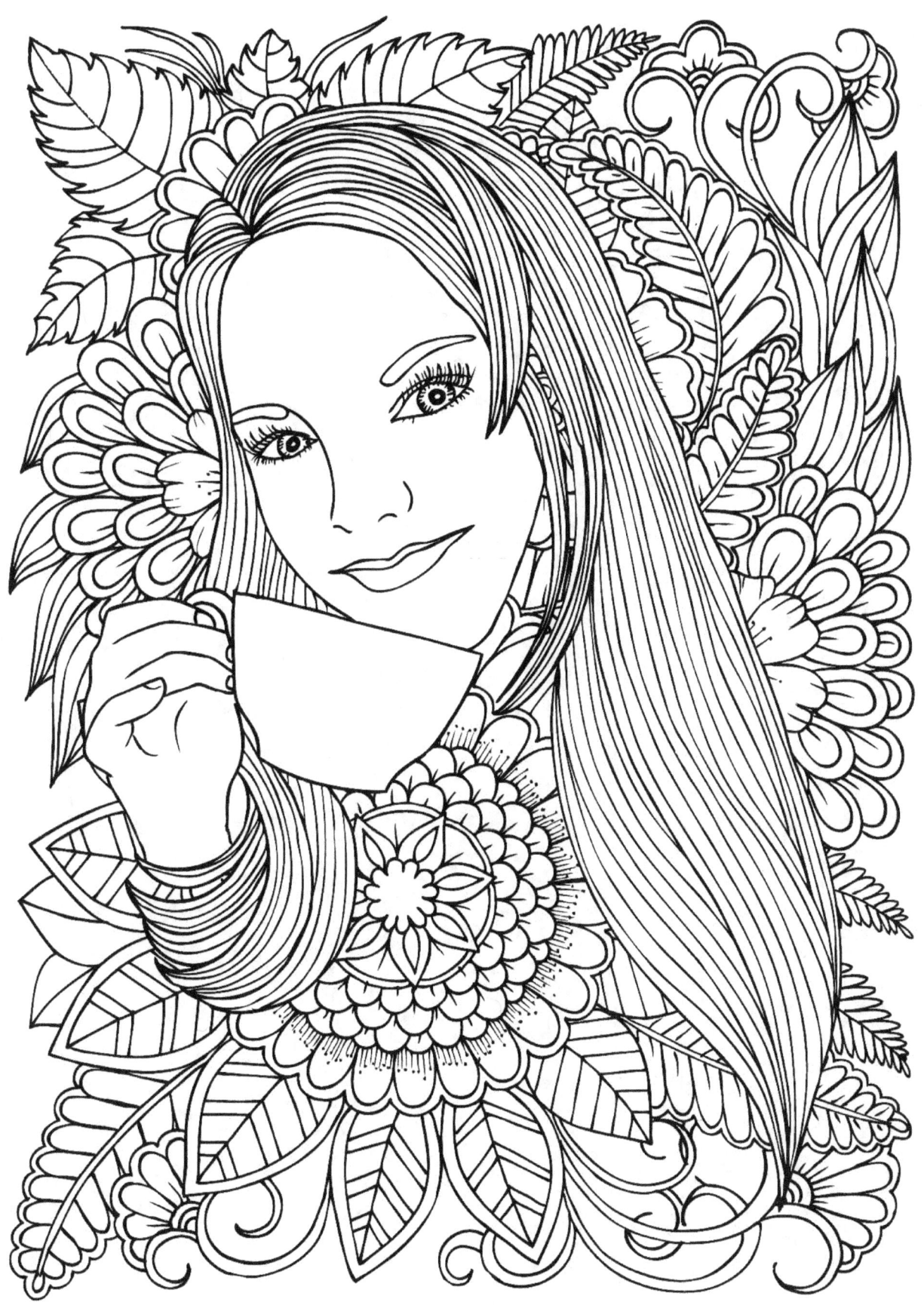

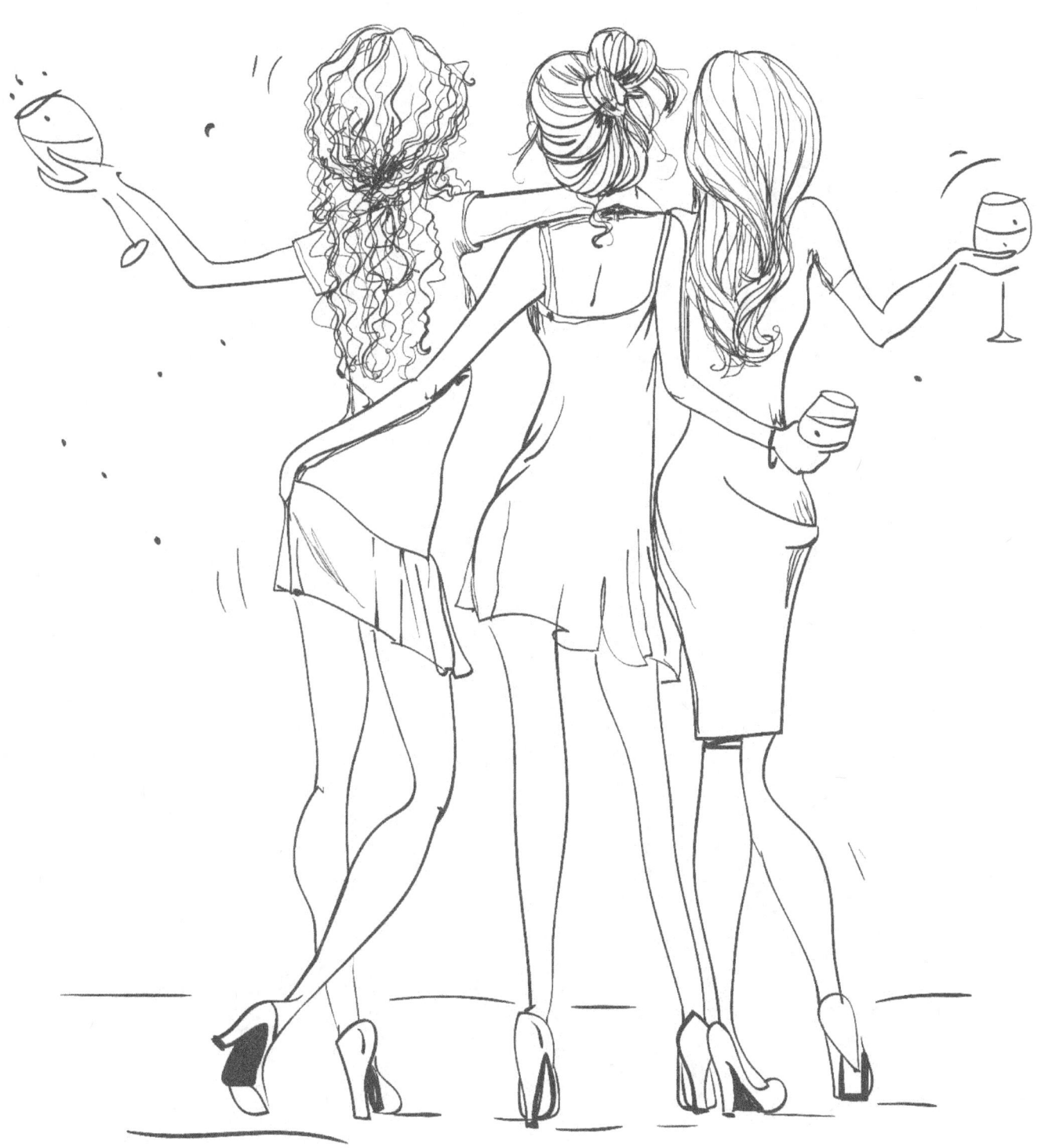

# FROM THE AUTHOR

Thanks for coloring our book! I hope it was relaxing and I hope you had a lot of fun with it.
We are waiting for you at the next coloring book.
A small favor, if you have a minute leave a comment on Amazon.
Thanks! See you soon.

*Talanova Liudmila Coloring Books*

www.ingramcontent.com/pod-product-compliance
Lightning Source LLC
Chambersburg PA
CBHW081432220526
45466CB00008B/2358